The Holy Spirit

by Heath Rogers

OneStone
BIBLICAL RESOURCES

Published by:
One Stone Press
979 Lovers Lane
Bowling Green, KY 42103

Printed in the United States of America

ISBN 10: 1-941422-08-X
ISBN 13: 978-1-941422-08-3

Supplemental Materials Available:
PowerPoint slides for each lesson
Answer key
Downloadable PDF

ONE STONE
BIBLICAL RESOURCES

www.onestone.com

Introduction

The Holy Spirit is a difficult subject. As a younger preacher I was intimidated by the subject and sometimes avoided preaching on it. I am confident that other preachers and Bible class teachers have done the same thing. This lack of teaching has created a void. Brethren naturally have questions about the Holy Spirit, and unfortunately they have gone to unreliable sources to satisfy their need for answers. As a result, it is not surprising to find Christians holding false views regarding the Holy Spirit. I have heard Christians make numerous false claims regarding the Holy Spirit. Some deny His deity. Some brethren have actually claimed the miraculous gifts of the Holy Spirit continue to exist today. I have heard brethren claim the Holy Spirit is speaking to and guiding them separate and apart from the word of God. A need for "instructive" teaching on the Holy Spirit has, in some places, turned into a need for "corrective" teaching on the Holy Spirit.

Because it is a difficult and controversial subject, I have often expected the sermons I would preach on the Holy Spirit to be poorly received by brethren. I have discovered that the opposite is true. Brethren have expressed sincere appreciation for the lessons that are found in this workbook. This tells me there is a true desire on the part of many brethren to learn what the Bible says about the Holy Spirit.

This workbook is not a textbook on the Holy Spirit. It is simply a tool to help one learn some things the Bible says about the Holy Spirit. The material does not address every passage that mentions the Holy Spirit. Neither does it address every possible question one may have about the Holy Spirit. It does, however, address many pertinent questions that are troubling brethren today. It can help one establish a foundation and perspective from which he can further study the subject if he so chooses. We must remember that the Bible itself does not answer every possible question about the Holy Spirit. Christians must learn that if the Bible does not provide an answer to our question, then God has not given us an answer. As with every subject, we must learn to be content with what the Bible does say, and not speculate about what it does not say.

I express my appreciation to the Robison Street church of Christ in Edna, TX, the Knollwood church of Christ in Beavercreek, OH, the Westview church of Christ in Hamilton, OH, and the Woodland Hills church of Christ in Tulsa, OK, for providing me the opportunity to develop and present the sermons which eventually became the material for this workbook.

I am especially grateful to Bruce Reeves who took the time to proofread this material. Andy Alexander also provided much needed help with one of the lessons. Many of their suggestions have been included in this material, and it is a better workbook because of their input.

Unless otherwise noted, all Bible quotations are taken from the New King James Version.

Foreword

Understanding the nature of the Holy Spirit, as well as his work is not only critical to our relationship with God, but it is a refreshing and rewarding consideration. While it is true that some have been influenced by the errors common in the current religious climate, we should ever be impressed with the power and value of an honest and open study of the Word of God.

This work, in my estimation, fairly and equitably presents various perspectives with an emphasis on the revelation of Scripture. I do not know of a vital issue in the context of this subject that is not addressed. Brother Heath Rogers has succinctly and thoughtfully approached the questions that are common in a discussion of the Holy Spirit and His work. Lessons ranging from the deity of the Holy Spirit to the question of the blasphemy of the Holy Spirit will challenge and help those who are diligently pursuing a better understanding of the biblical presentation of this question. The insight of the author to strive to explain not only the teaching of the scriptures, but also the psychological process by which people wrongfully attribute the thoughts of their conscience to the Spirit I found to be extremely profitable.

As we continue to study the work and nature of the Holy Spirit it is my conviction that this book will contribute helpful perspectives to the overall discussion and dialogue regarding the teaching of the Bible on this controversial, but understandable subject. May God bless all those disciples who seek to surrender their lives to Christ by submitting to the gospel revealed by the Holy Spirit!

—*Bruce Reeves*

Table of Contents

1. Who is the Holy Spirit? 7

2. The Holy Spirit in the Old Testament 13

3. The Holy Spirit and the Word 19

4. The Holy Spirit, the Conscience of Man, and Emotionalism 25

5. The Holy Spirit and the Apostles 33

6. The Holy Spirit and Conversion 39

7. The Holy Spirit and the Christian 45

8. The Indwelling of the Holy Spirit 51

9. The Baptism of the Holy Spirit 57

10. The Miraculous Gifts of the Holy Spirit 65

11. Speaking in Tongues 71

12. The Gift of the Holy Spirit in Acts 2:38 79

13. Sins Against the Holy Spirit 87

This book is dedicated to my good friend, Rick Dunham, a man who has shown me how to help and encourage others, how to honor and defend the Lord's cause, how to accept the trials of life with faith and dignity, and how to laugh as much as possible while doing so.

Who is the Holy Spirit?

There are many contradicting beliefs, teachings, and opinions in the religious world concerning the Holy Spirit. Some believe they have been baptized in the Spirit and are empowered by Him to perform miraculous works. Others deny this can happen today. Some believe the Holy Spirit personally and literally dwells in them. Others teach this is impossible. Some insist the Holy Spirit is nothing more than an influence or a mere manifestation of God—that He is not real. Others confess Him as a distinct member of the Godhead.

The only things we can know for certain about the Holy Spirit are those things that have been revealed in the Word of God. When it comes to understanding the Holy Spirit, we must be content with the teachings of the Bible, as opposed to relying upon denominational doctrines, human opinions, and personal feelings. The purpose of this lesson is to examine what the Bible has to say about the identity of the Holy Spirit.

The Names of the Holy Spirit

While the following is not an exhaustive list, it does contain many of the names or designations given to the Holy Spirit in the Word of God.

- **The Holy Spirit/Ghost**—Luke 4:1
- **The Spirit**—Luke 4:1
- **The Spirit of God**—Gen. 1:2
- **The Spirit of the Lord**— Luke 4:18
- **The Helper/Comforter**—John 16:7
- **The Spirit of Truth**—John 16:13
- **The Spirit of Grace**—Heb. 10:29
- **The Good Spirit**—Neh. 9:20
- **The Spirit of the Living God**—2 Cor. 3:3
- **The Spirit of Your Father**—Matt. 10:20
- **Promise of the Father**—Acts 1:4
- **The Spirit of Christ**—Rom. 8:9
- **The Spirit of Jesus Christ**—Phil. 1:19
- **The Eternal Spirit**—Heb. 9:14
- **The Spirit of Life**—Rom. 8:2
- **The Spirit of Holiness**—Rom. 1:4

The Holy Ghost

The Holy Spirit is not a "ghost" in the modern use of the word. In 1611, when the King James Version was translated, the word "ghost" meant "the soul as the seat of life or intelligence; hence, the spirit of man, as distinguished from the body." Today the word carries the idea of a disembodied spirit or a spook. While the "Holy Ghost" is a scriptural and accurate designation, there is nothing "spooky" about the Holy Spirit.

pneuma

The Greek word for "a current of air, a spirit"

These names or designations tell us some important things about the Holy Spirit. For instance, we know that He is a spirit. The word "spirit" is translated from the Greek word *pneuma* which means "a current of air, a spirit." He is not flesh and blood; not a physical being but a spiritual being. Also, notice these designations connect the Holy Spirit with God, as well as with truth, grace, life, and holiness.

Who is the Holy Spirit?

The Holy Spirit is God (Acts 5:3-4). We know Jesus is deity because He exhibited all the attributes of deity. The Holy Spirit likewise exhibits all the attributes of deity.

- **Eternal**—Heb. 9:14
- **Omnipresent**—Ps. 139:7
- **Omnipotent**—Ps. 104:30
- **Omniscient**—1 Cor. 2:10-11
- **Prescient (having foreknowledge)**—Acts 1:16
- **Infinite Life**—Rom. 8:2
- **Infinite Love**—Rom. 15:30
- **Infinite Holiness**—Rom. 1:4

Another way we know Jesus is deity is by the works He performed (John 5:36, 10:25). The Holy Spirit accomplished works that could only be done by deity (Please note, these works will be discussed in greater detail in other lessons in this workbook).

- **Creation**—Gen. 1:2; Job 26:13; Ps. 104:30
- **Revelation of God's Will To Man**—1 Cor. 2:9-12; Eph. 3:3-5
- **Confirmation of God's Will and Servants**—Heb. 2:3-4; Matt. 12:28
- **Inspiration**—2 Pet. 1:20-21
- **Incarnation**—Matt. 1:18; Luke 1:35
- **Regeneration**—John 3:5; Titus 3:5
- **Sanctification**—2 Thess. 2:13
- **Intercession**—Rom. 8:26
- **Conviction**—John 16:8
- **Comfort**—John 14:16, 26; 15:26; 16:7

While these attributes and works identify the Holy Spirit as deity, the Bible also shows the Holy Spirit has all of the qualities, characteristics, and attributes of a person or an individual. The following are all things that a person can do. The Holy Spirit:

- **Hears**—John 16:13
- **Speaks**—John 16:13; 1 Tim. 4:1

- **Guides**—John 16:13
- **Teaches**—John 14:26
- **Reminds**—John 14:26
- **Forbids**—Acts 16:6-7
- **Comforts**—Acts 9:31
- **Searches**—1 Cor. 2:10
- **Strives**—Gen. 6:3

The following are all things that can be done to a person. The Holy Spirit can be:

- **Grieved**—Eph. 4:30
- **Insulted**—Heb. 10:29
- **Blasphemed**—Matt. 12:31
- **Lied To**—Acts 5:3-4
- **Resisted**—Acts 7:51

The following are all things that a person has. The Holy Spirit has a:

- **Mind**—Rom. 8:27
- **Affection**—Rom. 15:30
- **Knowledge**—1 Cor. 2:11
- **Will**—1 Cor. 12:11

These Scriptures help us see that the Holy Spirit is a distinct individual. The Bible does not refer to the Holy Spirit with an impersonal pronoun ("it"). The Holy Spirit is referred to with the masculine pronouns "He" and "His."

The Holy Spirit is a Distinct Member of the Godhead

The Holy Spirit is not a mere manifestation of the Father or the Son. He is not the Word, nor a divine influence. He is a distinct member of the Godhead: one with God the Father and with God the Son.

The term "Godhead" appears three times in the King James Version of the Bible (Acts 17:29; Rom. 1:20; Col. 2:9). This term refers to the quality or essence of being divine or being God. While the Bible teaches there is one God (Deut. 6:4), it also teaches the Godhead is made up of three distinct persons or individuals: the Father, the Son, and the Holy Spirit. They are all separate from one another (the Father is not the Son or the Spirit, etc.), yet they are all equally God.

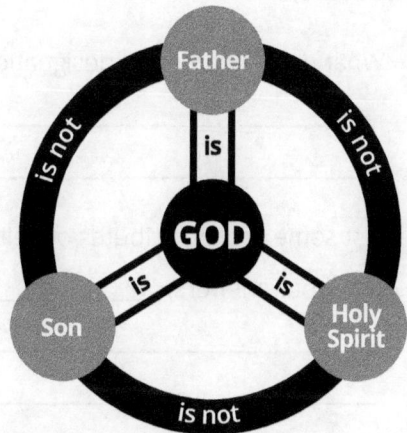

While this may be hard for us to understand, this Biblical concept is applied to more than just the Godhead. In the marriage relationship, the husband and wife are two separate individuals, yet they are joined together as "one flesh" (Gen. 2:24). The local church is made up of many members, yet they are one body (1 Cor. 12:12-27). Consider the apostles. Jesus prayed they would all be one, just as He and the Father are one (John 17:11). We understand the apostles were twelve distinct individuals, but they were united in power, purpose, authority, and action. Even so, the Godhead is made up of three distinct individuals, but they are united in power, purpose, authority, and action.

The Scriptures emphasize the fact that the members of the Godhead are distinct from each other. One example occurred when Jesus was baptized by John. When this event occurred, the Bible says the Father was in Heaven, the Son was on Earth, and the Spirit was seen descending upon the Son in the form of a dove (Matthew 3:13-17). There is no way the same individual could be three places at the same time.

The distinct nature of the members of the Godhead is also emphasized in the Lord's teaching on the Comforter (John 14:16-17; 15:26), the Great Commission (Matt. 28:19), the first gospel sermon preached by Peter (Acts 2:32-33), the assurance we have as children of God (Rom. 8:16-17), the great benediction (2 Cor. 13:14), and the three-fold witness (1 John 5:7, KJV, NKJV).

Conclusion

The Holy Spirit is not a divine influence or force extending from God the Father. He is a distinct member of the Godhead—equal in power and purpose with the Father and the Son. The Holy Spirit is a difficult subject, and as such we may understand less about Him than we do the Father and the Son. However, the Holy Spirit is a subject of the Bible. We must study to learn all we can about the third member of the Godhead, but we must also be content with what the Bible says about the nature and work of the Holy Spirit.

Questions

1. What do the names or designations of the Holy Spirit tell us about the Holy Spirit?

    _____

    _____

2. List some of the attributes of deity possessed by the Holy Spirit. Provide Scriptures with your answers. _____

    _____

    _____

3. How do the works performed by the Holy Spirit indicate He is deity?_____

    _____

    _____

4. How can we tell the Holy Spirit is a distinct individual, as opposed to an impersonal force?

    _____

    _____

5. What are some things the Holy Spirit can do? Provide Scriptures with your answers.

    _____

    _____

    _____

6. What are some things that can be done to the Holy Spirit? Provide Scriptures with your answers._____

    _____

    _____

7. What are some things the Holy Spirit has? Provide Scriptures with your answers.

    _____

    _____

    _____

8. What does the term "Godhead" mean? _____

    _____

9. How does the "oneness" of the apostles (John 17:11) help us understand how the Father, the Son, and the Holy Spirit can be one? _____

    _____

10. Describe how all three members of the Godhead were involved in the Lord's baptism (Matt. 3:13-17). _____

    _____

11. Describe how all three members of the Godhead were involved in the events of Pentecost (Acts 2:32-33). _____

    _____

    _____

The Holy Spirit in the Old Testament

Some people believe God the Father worked in the Old Testament, God the Son (Jesus Christ) was active only during the time He was upon the earth, and God the Spirit (the Holy Spirit) has only been active during the Gospel dispensation. According to the Bible, all three members of the Godhead have worked together in every dispensation of the world. While there has been diversity in their function, there has always been unity in their purpose (John 5:17, 10:30).

Although His role may appear to be more prominent in the New Testament, the Holy Spirit is mentioned as an active participant throughout the Old Testament. In this lesson we will consider some specific things the Holy Spirit accomplished during the time period of the Old Testament.

His Work in Creation

"In the beginning God created the heavens and the earth. The earth was without form, and void; and darkness was on the face of the deep. And the Spirit of God was hovering over the face of the waters" (Gen. 1:1-2).

The Hebrew word for "God" found in this passage is *elohim*. This word is a plural form of the Hebrew word for God—*el*. As we pointed out in the previous lesson, the Godhead consists of three equal persons—the Father, the Son, and the Holy Spirit. All three members of the Godhead were present and active during the creation of the world.

Although the Holy Spirit is present in the Hebrew term *elohim*, the Bible goes on to give some specific areas in which the Holy Spirit was involved in the creation of the world. The Holy Spirit was involved on the fourth day of creation in which the stars were placed in the heavens—"By His Spirit He adorned the heavens" (Job 26:13).

The Holy Spirit was involved when man was created on the sixth day. "Then God said, 'Let **Us** make man in **Our** image, according to **Our** likeness; let them have dominion over the fish of the sea, over the birds of the air, and over the cattle,

The Spirit of God—God or the Holy Spirit?

Several passages in the Old Testament speak of the "Spirit of God." For instance, Genesis 1:2 says "the Spirit of God was hovering over the face of the waters." The question is sometimes raised, "Is this God the Father's own personal Spirit or is it the Holy Spirit?"

Isaiah 48:16 helps to clarify this matter. The verse reads, "Come near to Me, hear this: I have not spoken in secret from the beginning; from the time that it was, I was there. And now the Lord God and His Spirit have sent Me." Notice a distinction is made between the "Lord God" and "His Spirit"—indicating they are two separate persons. So, the "Spirit of God" should be understood as the Holy Spirit, not God the Father (see also Isaiah 42:1-2, 61:1-3; Matt. 12:18).

over all the earth and over every creeping thing that creeps on the earth.' So God created man in His own image; in the image of God He created him; male and female He created them" (Gen. 1:26-27, emphasis mine—HR). Those who deny the triune nature of the Godhead claim that God was talking to the angels when He said, "Let Us make man in Our image," but the angels are not credited with the creation of man. Obviously God the Father was talking to the other two members of the Godhead, which means both the Son and the Holy Spirit played a role in the creation of man. As Elihu answered Job, he confessed, "The Spirit of God has made me, and the breath of the Almighty gives me life" (Job 33:4).

When man sinned, the Holy Spirit was involved in casting him from the Garden of Eden and the presence of the Tree of Life "Then the Lord God said, 'Behold, the man has become like one of **Us**, to know good and evil. And now, lest he put out his hand and take also of the tree of life, and eat, and live forever'—therefore the Lord God sent him out of the garden of Eden to till the ground from which he was taken" (Gen. 3:22-23, emphasis mine—HR).

The Holy Spirit is also the means by which God renews the vegetation of the earth. "You send forth Your Spirit, they are created; and You renew the face of the earth" (Ps. 104:30). The Holy Spirit began this work on the third day of creation, and it continues to the present day.

His Work of Inspiration

"Knowing this first, that no prophecy of Scripture is of any private interpretation, for prophecy never came by the will of man, but holy men of God spoke as they were moved by the Holy Spirit" (2 Peter 1:20-21).

The prophets of the Old Testament did not speak or write their own words or thoughts. They spoke or wrote as they were moved or carried along by the Holy Spirit. The prophet Balaam gives a good understanding of how the Holy Spirit inspired the prophets. Balak wanted to hire Balaam to curse the children of Israel (Num. 22:5-6). Balaam told Balak what he would be able to speak: "The word that God puts in my mouth, that I must speak" (v. 38). The Holy Spirit came upon Balaam, and Balaam spoke the words that he heard (Num. 24:2-4). Balaam blessed Israel. When challenged by Balak, Balaam defended his prophecy by saying, "What the Lord says, that I must speak" (v. 13). Inspiration did not consist of

And Balaam said to Balak, "Look, I have come to you! Now, have I any power at all to say anything? The word that God puts in my mouth, that I must speak."

- Num. 22:38

God giving the prophet the general idea, or the "germ" of truth, and allowing the prophet to develop the thought on his own. When a prophet was inspired by the Holy Spirit he was given the very words he was to speak or write.

All of the prophets spoke by the Holy Spirit. Among them were Moses and the seventy elders of Israel (Num. 11:24-25), King Saul (1 Sam. 10:6, 10-11), King David (Acts 1:16; 2 Sam. 23:2; Ps. 51:11), Isaiah (Acts 28:25), Ezekiel (Ezek. 11:5), and the unknown psalmist (Heb. 3:7-8; Ps. 95:7-11).

All Scripture is inspired by God (2 Tim. 3:16-17). The entire Old Testament was written by men who were inspired or moved along by the Holy Spirit.

His Workings With Mankind

The work of the Holy Spirit was not limited to "behind the scenes" activities such as creation or inspiration. He was very much involved in the lives of several individuals in the Old Testament.

The Holy Spirit strove with the wickedness of man during the days of Noah (Gen. 6:3). Noah is called a "preacher of righteousness" (2 Pet. 2:5). We are not told anything about the "preaching" Noah did, but there is no doubt that Holy Spirit was involved in this "preaching."

The Holy Spirit interpreted dreams. Joseph was called forth from prison to interpret Pharaoh's dream. Joseph said, "It is not in me; God will give Pharaoh an answer of peace" (Gen. 41:16). After he heard the interpretation, Pharaoh said of Joseph, "Can we find such a one as this, a man in whom is the Spirit of God?" (v. 38).

When it came time to construct the articles and garments needed for the service in the Tabernacle, the Holy Spirit filled men with wisdom, understanding, knowledge, and workmanship (Ex. 31:1-5) so they would know exactly how to construct these items.

During the period of the judges, the Holy Spirit sometimes fell upon men to give them extraordinary power:

- **Othniel**—Judg. 3:9-11
- **Gideon**—Judg. 6:34
- **Jephthah**—Judg. 11:29
- **Samson**—Judg. 14:5-6

> And the Lord said, "My Spirit shall not strive with man forever, for he is indeed flesh; yet his days shall be one hundred and twenty years."
>
> - Gen. 6:3

Solomon is credited with building the great Temple to God in Jerusalem. However, the plans for the Temple were given to his father David through the Holy Spirit (1 Chron. 28:11-13).

The Holy Spirit gathered nations for judgment (Is. 34:16) and brought destruction upon nations (Is. 59:19).

The Holy Spirit revealed the will of God to Ezekiel through visions and dreams (Ezek. 8:3, 11:1, 24-25), who in turn spoke these things to the people.

The Holy Spirit was involved in the restoration of Israel after Babylonian captivity (Ezek. 36:27-28, 37:14).

The Holy Spirit was instrumental in rebuilding the Temple (Zech. 4:6-9). The Temple was not rebuilt by the might or power of the Jews, but by the power and wisdom of the Holy Spirit.

Conclusion

Some believe each member of the Godhead had their own specific age or dispensation in which they did their work. They claim the Father was prominent in the Old Testament, Jesus was prominent while He was upon the earth, and the Holy Spirit did His work after Jesus ascended into heaven. The Holy Spirit may be mentioned more in the New Testament, but the Bible shows that He was very active in the Old Testament. He was present and involved in the creation of the world and man. He inspired the prophets as God began to reveal His will to man. Finally, the Holy Spirit worked directly in the lives of individuals and in the affairs of entire nations as God began to work through the descendants of Abraham to bring the Savior into the world.

Questions

1. How do we know the Holy Spirit is present in the first verse of the Bible? _____

    _____

    _____

2. What do the following verses teach regarding the Holy Spirit's involvement in creation?

    Job 26:13 _____

    Job 33:4 _____

    Psalm 104:30 _____

3. Who was God the Father talking to when He said, "Let Us make man in Our image, according to Our likeness" (Gen. 1:26)? _____

    _____

4. Using the example of Balaam (Num. 22:5-6, 38, 24:2-4, 13), explain how the Holy Spirit inspired the prophets. _____

_____

_____

5. How does David describe the Holy Spirit working through him (2 Sam. 23:1-2)? ____

_____

_____

6. What request did David make of God in Psalm 51:11?_____

_____

_____

7. According to the book of Hebrews, who wrote Psalm 95 (Heb. 3:7)? _____

_____

8. What did Pharaoh acknowledge about Joseph (Gen. 41:38)?_____

_____

9. What role did the Holy Spirit play in the construction of the Tabernacle (Ex. 31:1-5)?

_____

_____

10. What role did the Holy Spirit play in the construction of the Temple (1 Chron. 28:11-13)?

_____

_____

The Holy Spirit and the Word

The religious world abounds with false ideas about how the Holy Spirit works in the life of a Christian. These theories have arisen, in part, from a misunderstanding of the relationship between the Holy Spirit and the word of God. As we have seen in a previous lesson, the Holy Spirit is not the word. He is an individual part of the Godhead. However, in order to properly understand how the Holy Spirit works in influencing and helping mankind today, we must understand the Holy Spirit's relationship to the word of God.

The Revelation of the Will of God

The Holy Spirit plays an important role in the revelation of God's will to mankind. God has revealed His existence in His creation (Ps. 19:1; Rom. 1:18-20). We can know God exists, but we are not capable of knowing the will of God on our own. We need help. The Holy Spirit has searched the mind of God and has revealed His will to us through "words" we can understand (1 Cor. 2:9-13; Eph. 3:3-5).

"All Scripture is given by inspiration of God, and is profitable for doctrine, for reproof, for correction, for instruction in righteousness" (2 Tim. 3:16). The phrase "inspiration of God" is translated from a Greek word that literally means "God breathed." Thus, every word of the Bible has come from the mouth of God. It was the Holy Spirit who communicated these words to men who wrote them down as Scripture.

The words of the prophets were provided by the Holy Spirit (2 Pet. 1:21). The words of the apostles were likewise provided by the Holy Spirit (Matt. 10:19-20; John 16:12-15). These men were able to speak and write the word of God because the Holy Spirit guided them in the process of revelation. In fact, the Holy Spirit was not delivering His own words, but those things that had been given to Him by Jesus Christ (John 6:13-15). We would not have the word of God if it were not for the Holy Spirit.

> For prophecy never came by the will of man, but holy men of God spoke as they were moved by the Holy Spirit.
>
> - 2 Pet. 1:21

Revelation and Confirmation

The Holy Spirit empowered the apostles and other evangelists to perform miracles to confirm the words they spoke (Mark 16:20). These miracles, wonders, and signs sometimes generated an emotional response in individuals, but the purpose of these signs was to point the observer to the words that were being spoken. These individuals were guided through the word, not their emotions. The work of revelation and confirmation will be discussed in more detail in chapter ten.

The Holy Spirit Speaks To Man Through Words, Not Feelings

As we study through the Bible, we see a consistent pattern—the Holy Spirit speaks to men through words. It is important for us to make this observation. Many people today who believe they are being led by the Holy Spirit will offer their feelings as evidence of this leading. When the Holy Spirit sought to influence people, He spoke to them in words they could clearly understand, not in subjective emotions or feelings that could be misinterpreted.

- The Holy Spirit gave Philip clear instructions (Acts 8:29).

- The Holy Spirit gave Peter clear instructions (Acts 10:19-20).

- The Holy Spirit gave a specific prophecy to Agabus (Acts 11:27-28).

- The Holy Spirit spoke and gave instructions to the church in Antioch regarding Barnabas and Saul (Acts 13:2).

- The Holy Spirit witnessed that bonds and afflictions awaited Paul (Acts 20:22-23).

- Agabus testified as to what the Spirit had said concerning Paul (Acts 21:10-11).

- The Holy Spirit teaches the will of God in words (1 Cor. 2:13).

- The Holy Spirit spoke expressly concerning the latter days (1 Tim. 4:1).

We can see how the Holy Spirit guided these men. The Holy Spirit did not "lay something upon their hearts." They did not "feel" like the Holy Spirit was leading them in a particular direction. When the Holy Spirit led men He spoke directly to them in words they could understand.

The Holy Spirit and the Word of God— Their Influence Upon Mankind

The Holy Spirit and the word of God are inseparable and identical in their action upon the hearts of men. Whatever is affirmed of the Holy Spirit is also true of the word of God.

Action	Holy Spirit	Word of God
Witnesses	Rom. 8:16; John 15:26	John 5:39
Teach, instruct	John 14:26	2 Tim. 3:15-17
Convince, convict	John 16:8	Titus 1:9
Give birth	John 3:5, 8	James 1:18; 1 Pet. 1:23
Save man	Titus 3:5	James 1:21; Acts 11:14
Sanctify man	Rom. 15:16	John 17:17; Eph. 5:26
Cleanse man	1 Cor. 6:11	John 15:3; Eph. 5:26
Justify man	1 Cor. 6:11	Gal. 2:16 (Rom. 10:17)
Dwells in man	Rom. 8:9	Col. 3:16
Comfort	Acts 9:31	Rom. 15:4
Leads, guides	Rom. 8:14	Ps. 119:105
Has power	Rom. 15:13; Eph. 3:16	Rom. 1:16
Gives hope	Rom. 15:13	Rom. 15:4
Truth	John 14:17; 1 John 5:6	John 17:17
Gives life	John 6:63	John 6:68; Ps. 119:50, 93
Gives liberty	2 Cor. 3:17	John 8:32
Calls	Rev. 22:17	2 Thess. 2:14
Bears fruit	Gal. 5:22-23	Luke 8:11, 15
Walk in	Gal. 5:16, 25	2 John 6

The Holy Spirit and the word of God perform the same work upon man. Because of this, we understand the word of God is the instrument or medium through which the Holy Spirit preforms His work upon the hearts and minds of men today. In our first lesson, we learned that the Holy Spirit speaks, guides, teaches, reminds, forbids, and comforts man. He does this through His word. The word of God is said to be a **sword** (Eph. 6:17; Heb. 4:12), a **fire** (Jer. 23:29), a **hammer** (Jer. 23:29), a **seed** (Luke 8:11), and a **mirror** (James 1:22-25). The Holy Spirit uses the word as one would use a sword, a fire, a hammer, etc., as He guides, teaches, reminds, and comforts us today.

Consequences of the Holy Spirit Working Separate and Apart From the Word

Some people insist the Holy Spirit guides them separate and apart from the word of God. Unfortunately, our own brethren are sometimes heard to make this claim. This is not a harmless opinion. A belief in the direct working of the Holy Spirit separate from the word of God opens a dangerous door. Consider some of the consequences of this belief.

1. **The word of God is insufficient.** If the Holy Spirit is working upon my heart separate from the word of God, then He must supply something the word of God does not supply. However, the word of God is the power of God to salvation to everyone (Rom. 1:16), and it makes the man of God "complete, thoroughly equipped for every good work" (2 Tim. 3:16-17).

2. **Miracles have not ceased.** Any time deity interacts directly with man it is a miracle. If the Holy Spirit is "laying things upon our heart," whispering instructions in our ear, causing us to see visions, etc., we are experiencing miracles.

3. **If the Holy Spirit operates separate and apart from the word in a non-miraculous way, how do we know when the Holy Spirit is working?** Such understanding is subjective; that is, it is subject to the feelings of the individual. One believes the Holy Spirit is speaking to him simply because he "feels" like the Holy Spirit is speaking to him. This places one's emotions and feelings above and beyond the word of God. As we have seen in this lesson, the Holy Spirit never worked through the feelings of an individual. He spoke with words.

4. **What does the Holy Spirit do?** If the Holy Spirit works directly upon us separate and apart from the Holy Spirit, what does He do for us?

   - We know the Holy Spirit does not give us new revelation. The word of God has already been delivered in its entirety (Jude 3).

   - Some claim the Holy Spirit has to empower the word so it can work in our lives.[1] However, the Bible says the word of God is "living and powerful" (Heb. 4:12). It does not have to be "assisted" or "empowered" by the Holy Spirit.

   - The Holy Spirit does not have to interpret the word for us. The word of God has been delivered in a way that can be understood (Eph. 3:3-4, 5:17). The Holy Spirit performed His work through those men who wrote the Scriptures. The miraculous work of the Holy Spirit was done through the writers, not the readers.

   - The Holy Spirit does not guide us in making the trivial decisions of everyday life.

---

[1] "Unaccompanied by the power of the Holy Spirit, the Bible is inactive, inoperative; a mere dead letter! Apart from the Spirit, it cannot quicken, nor sanctify, nor comfort. It may be read constantly, and searched deeply, and known accurately, and understood partially, and quoted appropriately. Yet, left to its own unassisted power, 'it comes but in word only,' producing no hallowing, no abiding, no saving results" (Octavius Winslow, *The Glory of the Redeemer*, 1844, p. 347).

The Holy Spirit plays an important role in the life of a Christian, and these things will be studied in more detail in lesson seven. However, it is important for us to understand the Holy Spirit does not influence or speak to man separate and apart from the word of God.

Conclusion

There are many things about the Holy Spirit that are mysterious to us. We know the Holy Spirit plays a role in our life, but sometimes Christians are not certain what this role is. In the absence of good study and teaching, it is easy to allow the errors of the religious world to fill this void and believe the Holy Spirit is personally guiding us in a direct, miraculous, better-felt-than-told way. However, the Bible does speak on how the Holy Spirit influences mankind today. He speaks to us through His word.

Questions

1. What role does the Holy Spirit play in the revelation of God's will to mankind (1 Cor. 2:9-13)? _____

_____

2. What does the phrase "inspiration of God" (2 Tim. 3:16) literally mean, and what does it say about the word of God? _____

_____

_____

3. Who gave the inspired words to the prophets and apostles (2 Pet. 1:21; John 16:12-15)?

_____

4. Who gave these words to the Holy Spirit (John 16:13-15)? _____

5. What did the Holy Spirit say to Philip (Acts 8:29)? _____

_____

6. What did the Holy Spirit say to Peter (Acts 10:19-20)? _____

_____

7. What did the Holy Spirit say to the church in Antioch (Acts 13:2)? _____

_____

8. Did the Holy Spirit ever communicate His will to mankind through feelings or emotional experiences? _____

9. Explain how God's word is like the following items, and how the Holy Spirit would use God's word as these items:

    Sword (Eph. 6:17; Heb. 4:12) _____

    _____

    Fire (Jer. 23:29) _____

    _____

    Hammer (Jer. 23:29) _____

    _____

    Seed (Luke 8:11; 1 Pet. 1:23)_____

    _____

    Mirror (James 1:22-25)_____

    _____

10. What is the word of God able to do for us (2 Tim. 3:17)? _____

    _____

11. How do we know the Holy Spirit is not giving us new or additional revelation today (Jude 3)?_____

    _____

12. Does the Holy Spirit have to "empower" the word of God before it can work in our life (Heb. 4:12; Isa. 55:10-11)? _____

13. Can we understand the word of God, or do we need the Holy Spirit to interpret it for us (Eph. 3:3-4, 5:17)?_____

The Holy Spirit, the Conscience of Man, and Emotionalism

In 2006, the Richland Hills church of Christ in Fort Worth, Texas, made "history" by incorporating the use of instrumental music in their worship. In a sermon delivered on December 10, 2006, preacher Rick Atchley made the following statement regarding one of his reasons for making this departure from the New Testament pattern for worship:

> "Right there at that spot about 1994 **the Holy Spirit said to me in the middle of my sermon**, 'and that's what you and all the preachers like you were doing, who haven't for years believed that the worship of God with instruments is wrong. But you continue by your silence to let people think it's wrong, to allow the body to be disrupted, and you do so under the plea, "Well, we're just maintaining peace." But that's not peace; that's cowardice.' I knew then the day would come I'd have to teach this lesson" (Miller 5; emphasis added).

Atchley claims the Holy Spirit spoke directly to him as he was preaching a sermon. Denominational pastors make these kinds of claims all the time, but Atchley is a preacher for an institutional church of Christ.

The Holy Spirit is an avoided and misunderstood subject in the Lord's Church today. Brethren naturally have questions about the Holy Spirit. When there is a lack of teaching done on the Holy Spirit, brethren will sometimes fill this void with the errors they hear from their friends and neighbors and television preachers. More and more, we are hearing brethren claim to be led by the Holy Spirit separate and apart from His word. This can be heard in conversations and read on blogs and exchanges on social media. They are heard to make the same statements made by those in denominationalism: "The Holy Spirit spoke this to me." "The Holy Spirit laid this on my heart." "The Holy Spirit moved me." Like Atchley, sometimes these claims are used as a means of justifying a departure from the truth of God's

When there is a lack of teaching done on the Holy Spirit, brethren will sometimes fill this void with the errors they hear from their friends and neighbors and television preachers.

word. Thus we can see that teaching is needed on this important aspect of the Holy Spirit.

In our previous lesson, we learned that the Holy Spirit speaks to us and guides us through the Scriptures; the inspired and written word of God. What are we to believe regarding the claims by brethren that the Holy Spirit speaks to us directly, or guides our lives in a miraculous way? To address this question, we will study the conscience of man, the consistency of God's revelation, and emotionalism.

The Conscience of Man

God has supplied man with a conscience. The conscience is defined as "a knowledge or sense of right and wrong, with a compulsion to do right; moral judgment that opposes the violation of a previously recognized ethical principle and that leads to feelings of guilt if one violates such a principle" (Webster's Dictionary, 302).

Our conscience is our "guidance system." It lets us know if we are doing right or wrong. For instance, when we are doing what we understand to be wrong, our conscience will make us feel guilty. When we are doing what we understand to be right, our conscience will justify us or make us feel right. This is what Paul spoke of when he said one's conscience would either condemn or excuse his behavior (Rom. 2:15).

> Then Paul, looking earnestly at the council, said, "Men and brethren, I have lived in all good conscience before God until this day."
>
> - Acts 23:1

Each of us responds to our personal conscience. It is a guide, but it is only a safe guide if it has been properly trained according to the standards set forth in God's word. Paul made it his aim to have a pure conscience before God and man (Acts 23:1, 24:16). He persecuted the church with a clear conscience because he believed it was the right thing for him to do (Acts 26:9). He was wrong. Even though he was acting with a clear conscience he was actually opposing the will of God. When he learned the truth, he changed his understanding of right and wrong, and preached the gospel of Jesus Christ with a clear conscience.

The conscience of the Christian is trained by the word of God. The apostle Paul said, "And do not be conformed to this world, but be transformed by the **renewing of your mind**, that you may prove what is that good and acceptable and perfect will of God" (Rom. 12:2, emphasis mine—HR). Our way of thinking is "transformed" when our minds are renewed. This is not done miraculously. Our minds are renewed as we learn God's standards of right and wrong set forth in His word. As we learn these standards of righteousness, our conscience is trained.

The Christian must allow his conscience to be trained by the word of God, and not by family traditions, personal opinions, worldly standards, or denominational doctrines. The conscience cannot be a safe guide if it has been trained by a false standard.

"Your word I have hidden in my heart, that I might not sin against You" (Ps. 119:11). If we have trained our conscience by filling our hearts with the word of God, our conscience will remind us of these Scriptures as we face challenges and make decisions throughout the day. When we see someone in need, we will feel moved to help them, not because the Holy Spirit is "laying that on our heart," but because we know it is the right thing to do. When we contemplate making a bad decision, we will feel a sense of guilt or disapproval regarding that decision. This is not the Holy Spirit making us feel bad. It is our conscience doing its job.

Much of the work attributed to the Holy Spirit is actually the work of man's conscience. Consider again the statement made by Rick Atchley. He claimed the Holy Spirit spoke to him while he was preaching a sermon, but notice the message he supposedly received from the Holy Spirit. The Holy Spirit did not tell him it was all right to use the instrument. The Holy Spirit supposedly condemned Atchley of "cowardice" for refusing to preach what he believed to be the truth regarding the use of the instrument. This was not the Holy Spirit talking to Atchley. It was his conscience speaking to him; condemning him for doing something he believed to be wrong.

The Holy Spirit Cannot Contradict the Word of God

People who claim to receive miraculous guidance from the Holy Spirit often uphold doctrines and practices which are contrary to Scripture. When the inconsistency between their belief and the teaching of Scripture is pointed out, they will sometimes respond with statements such as, "I would rather have what I feel in my heart than what is written in a whole stack of Bibles," or, "A person with an experience is never at the mercy of a person with an argument." Such individuals give their feelings and experiences more merit

> Much of the work attributed to the Holy Spirit is actually the work of man's conscience.

There is one body and one Spirit, just as you were called in one hope of your calling.

- Eph. 4:4

than the word of God. Although they may not acknowledge it, they are, in fact, elevating themselves above God's word.

1. **The Bible warns man not to trust in his heart.** Such individuals rely heavily upon the feelings of their own heart. The Bible gives strong warnings against this. "The heart is deceitful above all things, and desperately wicked; who can know it?" (Jer. 17:9). "There is a way that seems right to a man, but its end is the way of death" (Prov. 14:12).

2. **God does not contradict Himself.** "For I am the Lord, I do not change..." (Mal. 3:6). "Jesus Christ is the same yesterday, today, and forever" (Heb. 13:8). The Holy Spirit is never going to give us a message or lead us into something that is contrary to the word of God.

3. **God is not the author of confusion.** "For God is not the author of confusion but of peace, as in all the churches of the saints" (1 Cor. 14:33). Those who claim to receive direct guidance from the Holy Spirit often believe contradicting doctrines. How is this possible? The Holy Spirit would not reveal one thing to one person, and something different to another. If they are all led by the same Spirit (Eph. 4:4) shouldn't they all be teaching and practicing the same things? Personal experiences are subjective, while God's word is an established standard. God's word (revealed by the Holy Spirit) sets forth the truth, not one's personal feelings, emotions, impulses, or experiences.

4. **The Bible tells us to test the spirits.** "Beloved, do not believe every spirit, but test the spirits, whether they are of God; because many false prophets have gone out into the world" (1 John 4:1). We are not to believe every teacher who comes our way. We are to test their teaching according to the word of God. Paul invited the Corinthians to put his instructions to the test (1 Cor. 14:37). This same test needs to be used by those who claim to have new teachings laid upon their hearts or whispered in their ears by the Holy Spirit. If what they are "hearing" from the Holy Spirit is not in accordance with the teaching of the Bible, it is not of God and must be rejected. Instead, the word of God is often rejected in favor of what they feel has been laid upon their heart.

Rick Atchley used a message he claimed to have received from the Holy Spirit as justification for employing instrumental music in worship. This is a departure from the pattern set forth in the New Testament, and thus cannot be from the Holy Spirit. If his claim has merit, what will stop a Christian from claiming the Holy Spirit told him to only observe the Lord's Supper once a year, that women can preach and serve as elders, that water baptism is not essential for salvation, etc.? God does not contradict His word.

Emotionalism

God has given man emotions. We have the ability to experience things such as love (1 Pet. 4:8), joy (Phil. 4:4), sorrow (2 Cor. 7:10), and fear (Matt. 10:28). While our emotions are important, God has also created us with the ability to reason and understand (Is. 1:18; Eph. 5:17).

Emotion has its place in our service and worship, but we must understand its place. Emotion does not create or establish truth. It is appropriate for man to have an emotional response when he gains knowledge of the truth. The Jews on Pentecost were cut to the heart (an emotional response) when they learned they were guilty of crucifying their Messiah (Acts 2:36-37). Felix became afraid when he heard Paul preach about righteousness, self-control, and the judgment to come (Acts 24:25). The Philippian Jailer rejoiced after he heard and obeyed the gospel (Acts 16:30-34).

Emotion is the proper response to knowledge, but emotion without understanding is not enough to please God. "Brethren, my heart's desire and prayer to God for Israel is that they may be saved. For I bear them witness that they have a zeal for God, but not according to knowledge" (Rom. 10:1-2). Israel had emotion, they had zeal, but they did not have knowledge of the truth. They were not saved.

Some religious people today are filled with zeal and enthusiasm, but they express little regard for the word of God. They would rather have an experience, or have the Holy Spirit lay something upon their heart, than be content to follow the words of the Bible. The Holy Spirit revealed the will of God to man. This knowledge will condemn man of his sin in an effort to bring him unto repentance. When man responds to the gospel in obedience, he can rejoice in the forgiveness of his sins. As he continues to abide in the doctrine of Christ, he will continue to find joy and peace. A personal and direct experience with the Holy Spirit is not necessary in order for one to feel these emotions, neither

"Come now, and let us reason together," says the Lord...

- Is. 1:18

are these emotional experiences evidence that one has had an experience with the Holy Spirit.

Conclusion

The Holy Spirit has revealed the will of God to man in words which we can understand. He influences man through the word of God. He does not speak directly to the hearts of men today. He speaks, teaches, warns, guides, etc., through the word of God.

Mankind has been created with a conscience which guides him in his life. If trained by the word of God, the conscience will warn man when he is doing wrong and approve man when he is doing right. If we will store up the word of God in our heart through Bible reading, study, and meditation, it will be available to us when we need it in our daily lives. The Holy Spirit does not guide us or miraculously remind us of Scripture in our daily lives. This is the work of our conscience.

Mankind has also been created with the ability to experience emotions. However, emotion is never the source of truth. Rather, knowledge of truth is what generates proper emotional responses. Religious emotionalism void of knowledge is not enough to save our soul or make us acceptable unto God.

References

Guralnik, David B. *Webster's New World Dictionary of the American Language*, New York, NY: 1986

Miller, Dave. *Richland Hills & Instrumental Music, A Plea to Reconsider*, Apologetics Press, Inc., Montgomery, AL, 2007, print

Questions

1. What is man's conscience? _____

    _____

2. How does our conscience "guide" us? _____

    _____

3. How can we make our conscience a safe guide? _____

    _____

4. Why did Paul have a pure and clear conscience when he was persecuting the church (Acts 26:9)? _____

    _____

    _____

5. In Romans 12:2, Paul spoke of the renewing of our minds. Explain how the mind of the Christian is "renewed." _____

    _____

    _____

6. Does the Bible encourage us to follow our heart (Jer. 17:9; Prov. 14:12)? Why or why not? _____

    _____

    _____

7. Will the Holy Spirit ever lead man in a way which is contrary to the word of God (Mal. 3:6)? _____

8. What must we do with any message which is contrary to God's word (Gal. 1:6-9)?

    _____

    _____

9. Describe the emotions felt when the following people heard the word of God:
    Jews on Pentecost (Acts 2:36-37) _____

    _____

    Felix (Acts 24:25) _____

    _____

    Philippian Jailer (Acts 16:30-34) _____

    _____

10. Is having emotion enough to make us acceptable before God (Rom. 10:1-2)? _____

    _____

The Holy Spirit and the Apostles

In order to properly understand the Bible we must rightly divide the Word of God (2 Tim. 2:15). While we are reading the Bible we must make note who is speaking and what he is saying, but we must also understand who is being spoken unto. Some passages in the Bible are universal in their application. Others apply only to specific groups or individuals. A failure to recognize this important distinction can result in us misunderstanding a portion of God's Word.

In John chapters 14-16, Jesus gave specific instructions and promises to the men He had chosen to be His apostles. These promises were great, but they were only given to these specific individuals. Some of the confusion and error that exists on the subject of the Holy Spirit results from a failure to make this important distinction. Some read the Lord's words given to the apostles and make application to themselves, without stopping to ask if these promises were meant for all Christians. In this lesson, we will examine these chapters and learn what the Holy Spirit was to do for the apostles.

John 14-16 is the Lord's "Farewell Address" to His apostles. It is the last time He spoke to them before His death. He was doing His best to prepare them, not only for His death, but also for His departure after His resurrection. He told them He was leaving them, which caused them sorrow. Jesus said it was actually to their advantage that He leave so He could send the Holy Spirit to them.

Jesus spoke of the Holy Spirit four times in these chapters (14:15-18, 26; 15:26-27; 16:7-15). It is in these verses that we learn what the Holy Spirit was to do for the apostles.

A Helper or Comforter (John 14:16-18)

Jesus was leaving them, but He was not deserting them as orphans. He would send "another Helper." This "Helper" was identified by the Lord as the "Spirit of truth" (v. 17) or the "Holy Spirit" (v. 26).

> And I will pray the Father, and He will give you another Helper, that He may abide with you forever—the Spirit of truth, whom the world cannot receive, because it neither sees Him nor knows Him; but you know Him, for He dwells with you and will be in you.
>
> - John 14:16-17

The Holy Spirit did not always intervene directly with the apostles. In Acts 15 men came to Antioch from Jerusalem and taught that the Gentiles had to be circumcised and keep the Law of Moses in order to be saved (v. 1). Paul and Barnabas traveled to Jerusalem to settle this matter. There they met with the apostles and elders of the church. Instead of the Holy Spirit falling upon them and revealing the truth, these men were allowed to present evidence which pointed to the indisputable fact that God had received the uncircumcised Gentiles (vs. 6-21). This sets the example we must follow today. We do not have this measure of the Holy Spirit that was given to the apostles, but we do have the Scriptures which equip us and guide us into all truth.

The word "helper," "comforter" (KJV) or "counselor" (NIV) is translated from the Greek word *parakletos*. There is no one English word that precisely expresses the meaning of *parakletos*. The word literally means "to call to one's side" or to give aid. A combination of the words used to translate *parakletos* can give us a better idea of the meaning of this Greek word. The word is used only five times in the New Testament. Four times it applies to the Holy Spirit (John 14:16, 26; 15:26; 16:7) and once it applies to Jesus Christ (1 John 2:1).

The Holy Spirit was given to the apostles as a unique gift. He was taking the place of Christ in their lives and their work as apostles. The Holy Spirit was "another Helper" who was comparable to their first Helper—Jesus. However, unlike Jesus, this Helper (the Holy Spirit) would not leave them, but would abide with them forever (14:16).

As we study the rest of the passages in these chapters, the Spirit's role as a helper or comforter becomes more understandable.

Teach All Things, Bring To Remembrance All Things (John 14:26)

The Helper or Comforter is said to equip the apostles with two things: inspired teaching and inspired memory.

The apostles were inspired by the Holy Spirit, and thus spoke and wrote by inspiration (1 Cor. 2:12-13). The early Christians "continued steadfastly in the apostles' doctrine" (Acts 2:42), which consisted of those things which were taught to the apostles by the Holy Spirit.

Human memory is subject to limitations, imperfections, and bias. However, the apostles did not have to rely upon themselves to call to mind the things the Lord had said and done among them. The Spirit supplied them with a perfect recollection of all the things Christ had personally taught them.

It is important to recognize that only the apostles were given this gift. Timothy, a man who possessed miraculous gifts of the Holy Spirit (2 Tim. 1:6), was told to study to show himself approved unto God (2 Tim. 2:15), which means he did not have this measure of the Spirit. Also, the apostles were told not to worry about how they would answer when brought before dignitaries and authorities, for the Holy Spirit would teach them what to say (Luke 12:11-12). However, the apostle Peter told Christians to always be ready to give an answer to every man who asks for the reason of their hope (1 Peter 3:15, KJV). It is obvious that we do not receive this measure of the Holy Spirit.

Testify of Christ (John 15:26-27)

The Holy Spirit is said to "testify" or "bear witness" of Christ. "Witness" is a much abused word in the religious world today. The only way one can bear witness of another or give testimony is if they have actually seen these things themselves.

Jesus told the apostles He would send the Holy Spirit to them, and the Spirit would take the things that are Christ's and would declare them to the apostles (16:14-15). The Holy Spirit did not have His own agenda, but continued the work that Christ began with the apostles.

Together with the Holy Spirit, the apostles were to bear witness to the world of the things they had seen and heard concerning Christ. An apostle had to be an eyewitness of the resurrected Lord (Acts 1:21-22). Together, the Holy Spirit and the apostles bore witness of the Lord's resurrection on Pentecost (Acts 2:32-33). While we can certainly tell others about the death of Christ and the salvation He offers, none of us are qualified to do the work of an apostle. The Holy Spirit is not working with us in the same way He worked with the apostles.

Convict the World of Sin, Righteousness, and Judgment (John 16:8-11)

To "convict" or "reprove" is to expose one's actions and prove that they are wrong. The Holy Spirit's work through the apostles of convicting the world of sin, righteousness, and judgment began on Pentecost when Peter's sermon vindicated Jesus Christ before the Jews who had crucified Him (Acts 2). In this sermon, the Holy Spirit convicted them of:

- **Sin**—"because they do not believe in Me" (v. 9). Their specific sin was not believing in Christ (Acts 2:22-24, 36).

- **Righteousness**—"because I go to the Father" (v. 10). The world was convicted of Jesus' righteousness. Jesus was charged with blasphemy and crucified because He claimed to be the Son of God. When God raised Him

> But when the Helper comes, whom I shall send to you from the Father, the Spirit of truth who proceeds from the Father, He will testify of Me.
>
> - John 15:26

from the dead, He ascended into Heaven to be with the Father and from there poured forth the Holy Spirit (Acts 2:32-33). This proved Jesus was who He claimed to be. He was righteous; innocent of the charge of blasphemy.

- **Judgment**—"because the ruler of this world is judged" (v. 11). When Jesus rose from the dead, Satan (the ruler of this world) was defeated. While the death of Christ would seem to be a victory for Satan, it was actually the means of his ultimate defeat (Heb. 2:14, John 12:31-32).

The words of the New Testament, given through the inspiration of the Holy Spirit, continue to convict the world of sin, righteousness, and the judgment to come.

Guide the Apostles into All Truth (John 16:12-13)

Jesus had not taught the apostles all the truth they needed to hear. They were not of a frame of mind to receive it all that evening. So, the Holy Spirit would be given to them to guide them into all truth.

Sometimes we encounter people who will only read the "red letters" of the Bible. Some Bibles print the words of Christ in red, and these individuals will only read and follow the words of Christ (the "red letters"). While this may appear to be a noble conviction, the reality is that Jesus Himself taught the "red letters" do not contain all the truth we need to hear. We must receive all the writings of the apostles and other Spirit-inspired writers of the New Testament as we would receive the words of Christ Himself.

Also, notice that the Holy Spirit did not reveal a portion of the truth to the apostles. He revealed "all truth." This fact does away with the need for and validity of latter-day revelations. The entire truth of the gospel has been "once for all delivered to the saints" (Jude 3).

Tell the Apostles of Things To Come (John 16:13)

The Holy Spirit also revealed some things to the apostles which were going to take place in the future.

- **The falling away** (2 Thess. 2:3, 1 Tim. 4:1-3)
- **The Second Coming of Christ** (1 Thess. 4:13-18)
- **The resurrection of the dead** (1 Cor. 15)
- **Triumph of the church over the Roman Empire** (Revelation)

Conclusion

The Lord made great promises to the apostles regarding the help they would receive from the Holy Spirit, but these promises were limited to the apostles. The Holy Spirit is not a Helper or Comforter for us in the sense He was for the apostles. However, we do receive much needed help and comfort from the work the Holy Spirit did through the apostles. As the Holy Spirit taught them all things, reminded them of all things, and guided them into all truth, they wrote it down. When we read what they wrote, we can understand all things that the Holy Spirit has given the apostles (Eph. 3:3-5).

Questions

1. Are the instructions and promises concerning the Holy Spirit in John 14-16 for all believers today? Why or why not? _____

   _____

   _____

2. What two things did the Holy Spirit provide for the apostles (John 14:26)? _____

   _____

3. Regarding the answer to the above question, what evidence shows that not all Christians were blessed with this measure of the Holy Spirit (2 Tim. 2:15; 1 Pet. 3:15)?

   _____

   _____

4. Did the Holy Spirit always miraculously guide the apostles in understanding or establishing the truth on all matters (Acts 15:6-21)? _____

5. Can anyone today bear witness of the resurrected Christ as did the apostles? Why or why not? _____

   _____

6. Of what three things would the Holy Spirit convict the world (John 16:8)? _____

   _____

   _____

7. How did the Holy Spirit convict the Jews of sin, righteousness, and judgment through the preaching of Peter in Acts 2?_____

   _____

8. How does the Holy Spirit convict the world today?_____

   _____

9. Did the Lord deliver all truth to the apostles on the night He was betrayed (John 16:12-13)?_____

10. Where can we go to learn "all truth?" _____
    _____

11. Jesus said the Holy Spirit would tell the apostles about "things to come" (John 16:13).
    What were some of these things?_____
    _____
    _____

12. How do we benefit from the work done by the Holy Spirit through the apostles?
    _____
    _____
    _____

The Holy Spirit and Conversion

It is the will of God that all men be saved and come to the knowledge of the truth (1 Tim. 2:3-4). God's great scheme of redemption is woven throughout the pages of the Bible. As we read the Bible, we learn that all three members of the Godhead, including the Holy Spirit, play important roles in securing man's salvation.

One must be born again in order to be saved (John 3:3-5). The Holy Spirit is involved in this new birth. When man is saved, he is regenerated or renewed by the Holy Spirit (Titus 3:5). Spiritually speaking, he is brought back to life, or is "born again" by the Holy Spirit.

Many people today believe man is saved through a "divine grace" resulting from a direct operation of the Holy Spirit upon the heart of sinners. They insist this operation takes place separate and apart from the word of God. This false teaching has its roots in Calvinism, which teaches:

> "Therefore, the Holy Spirit, in order to bring God's elect to salvation, extends to them a special inward call in addition to the outward call contained in the gospel message. Through this special call the Holy Spirit performs a work of grace within the sinner which inevitably brings him to faith in Christ." (Steele, Thomas 48-49).

Those choosing to follow this error base the certainty of their salvation upon their feelings. Instead of looking at what the Bible says, some of them will reject the plain teaching of the Bible in preference of their emotions and experiences.

The Holy Spirit is involved in man's conversion or salvation. The important questions are: "What does the Holy Spirit do to save man, and how does He do it?" The Bible answers these questions, and we must be satisfied with the way the Bible answers these questions.

The Word of God and Man's Salvation

God, in His divine wisdom, has seen fit to save man through the preaching of the gospel (1 Cor. 1:21). The medium

> Not by works of righteousness which we have done, but according to His mercy He saved us, through the washing of regeneration and renewing of the Holy Spirit...
>
> - Titus 3:5

through which God works to save man is His word, not through a miraculous, direct operation of the Holy Spirit. Consider the following passages of Scripture:

- "I do not pray for these alone, but also for those who will believe in Me through their word" (John 17:20).

- "And truly Jesus did many other signs in the presence of His disciples, which are not written in this book; but these are written that you may believe that Jesus is the Christ, the Son of God, and that believing you may have life in His name" (John 20:30-31)

- "And when there had been much dispute, Peter rose up and said to them: 'Men and brethren, you know that a good while ago God chose among us, that by my mouth the Gentiles should hear the word of the gospel and believe'" (Acts 15:7).

- "For I am not ashamed of the gospel of Christ, for it is the power of God to salvation for everyone who believes, for the Jew first and also for the Greek" (Rom. 1:16).

- "So then faith comes by hearing, and hearing by the word of God" (Rom. 10:17).

- "...receive with meekness the implanted word, which is able to save your souls" (James 1:21).

- "Having been born again, not of corruptible seed but incorruptible, through the word of God which lives and abides forever" (1 Pet. 1:23).

The Holy Spirit causes us to be born again through the word of God (Jn. 3:5; 1 Pet. 1:23). Since the Holy Spirit wrote or inspired the word, what the word does, the Spirit does through the medium of His word.

The gospel is God's power to salvation (Rom. 1:16). The gospel was delivered by the Holy Spirit who was sent from Heaven (1 Pet. 1:12). When inspired men preached the gospel, the Holy Spirit was working. The Holy Spirit continues to work when His inspired word is preached today.

Accounts of Conversion in Acts

The fact that the Holy Spirit works through the word of God to bring about man's conversion can be seen in the accounts of conversion found in the book of Acts.

Jesus answered, "Most assuredly, I say to you, unless one is born of water and the Spirit, he cannot enter the kingdom of God."

- John 3:5

1. 3,000 on Pentecost (Acts 2:1-4, 33-39)

- The Holy Spirit was poured out upon the apostles and they began to speak with other tongues as the Spirit gave them utterance.

- A multitude gathered and marveled at what they were seeing and hearing. Peter began to preach, telling them they were witnessing the fulfillment of a prophecy found in the book of Joel.

- Peter went on to tell them the pouring out of the Holy Spirit was evidence that God had made Jesus, whom they had crucified, both Lord and Christ.

- When they heard this, they were "cut to the heart" (v. 37). Jesus said the Holy Spirit would "convict" men of their sin (John 16:8). He did so on this occasion through the preaching of the gospel. When they asked what they had to do, Peter told them to repent and be baptized in the name of Jesus Christ for the remission of their sins (v. 38).

- The Holy Spirit was present on this occasion, but He was not interacting directly with those who were in need of salvation. He inspired Peter to preach the gospel and deliver the terms of salvation. They were saved when they obeyed what Peter told them to do.

2. The Ethiopian Eunuch (Acts 8:29, 39)

- The Holy Spirit spoke to Philip, telling him to go near and overtake the eunuch's chariot. He did so, preached the gospel, and baptized the eunuch. After the gospel had been preached, and the eunuch had been converted, the Holy Spirit reappeared in the account and snatched Philip away.

- Note that the Holy Spirit led the preacher to the sinner who was seeking the truth, but He did not interact directly with the man who was lost.

3. Cornelius (Acts 10:19-20, 44-48)

- Cornelius was a Gentile. An angel appeared to him and told him to send for Peter who would come and tell him what he must do in order to be saved.

- The following day, the Holy Spirit spoke to Peter, instructing him to go with the men who had come for him, doubting nothing.

> There are no examples of conversion or any statement in the New Testament indicating the Holy Spirit works directly upon the heart of a sinner separate and apart from the word of God.

- He went with them and preached to all those who were gathered at the house of Cornelius. As he spoke, the Holy Spirit fell upon the Gentiles, serving as a sign to Peter and the other Jewish Christians that the Gentiles were proper candidates for the gospel. After seeing this sign, Peter commanded them to be baptized.

The Holy Spirit is involved in all of these accounts of conversion, but He does not speak to or act directly upon any sinner. He speaks to the preacher who speaks the word of God to the sinner. The Holy Spirit works through the spoken word to convict the sinner and help him understand what he must do to be saved. The only exception is the outpouring of the Holy Spirit upon the household of Cornelius. A careful study of this account will show this was not done because the Gentiles were saved, nor was it done to help them accept the gospel. It was done for the benefit of Peter and the other Jewish Christians who were present.

The Holy Spirit works through the same medium (His word) to bring about the salvation of mankind today.

The Holy Spirit Brings About Man's Conversion

The word "conversion" suggests a change. When man is converted or saved from his sins, he undergoes a number of changes, and the Holy Spirit is involved in every one of these changes.

1. **A change in his heart.** A man's heart must change in order for him to be converted to the truth. His understanding and attitude towards God, the reality of his sin, and the call of the gospel, must change. It is the Holy Spirit who convicts man of his sin, righteousness, and judgment to come (John 16:8). This is done through the preaching of the gospel, which always brings about a change in a good and honest heart.

2. **A change in state or condition.** To be "born again" or "regenerated" means one has changed from spiritual death to spiritual life. It is the Holy Spirit who causes us to be born again or regenerated (John 3:3-5; Titus 3:5). This change occurs at the point of baptism (Rom. 6:3-4) of which the Holy Spirit plays a part (1 Cor. 12:13).

3. **A change in relationship.** One who is converted goes from being an enemy of God to enjoying fellowship with God. When we were lost in sin we were enemies with God (Rom. 5:8-10; Col. 1:21-22). We are reconciled and brought back into fellowship with God through the Holy Spirit (Eph. 2:18; 2 Cor. 13:14).

The Holy Spirit is present and active throughout our conversion. This work is done through the word of God, which is inspired by the Holy Spirit. Man is saved, not because he is overpowered by the Holy Spirit, but because he obeys the conditions of salvation set forth by the Holy Spirit in the word of God.

Conclusion

It is unfortunate that many people desire something more than what is promised in the word of God. Some have been made to believe they are saved because of a direct operation of the Holy Spirit upon their heart. It is difficult to reason with such people because they often elevate their feelings above the word of God.

The Scriptures clearly teach the Holy Spirit is involved in our salvation, and they teach how He is involved. He appeals to man through the word, not through miracles or emotions. Because of this, we can know we are saved, not because of our feelings, but because we have done what the Holy Spirit has said we must do.

References

Steele, David N., Thomas, Curtis C. "The Five Points of Calvinism: Defined, Defended, Documented" Phillipsburg, NJ, Presbyterian & Reformed Publishing Co. 1963

Questions

1. What important work is credited to the Holy Spirit in John 3:5 and Titus 3:5?_____

    _____

2. Through what means has God chosen to save mankind (1 Cor. 1:21)? Provide some other Scriptures to support your answer. _____

    _____

    _____

3. Through what medium does the Holy Spirit work to cause us to be born again (1 Pet. 1:23)? _____

4. Was the Holy Spirit involved in the accounts of conversion in the book of Acts?

    _____

5. Did the Holy Spirit ever speak directly to those who were lost and help them understand what they must do to be saved?_____

6. Why did the Holy Spirit fall upon the household of Cornelius (Acts 10:44-48, 11:15-18)?

    _____

    _____

7. State three changes that take place in man's conversion, and explain how the Holy Spirit is involved in these changes._____

    _____

    _____

The Holy Spirit and the Christian

So far in this study, we have considered many things the Holy Spirit has done in the past. He was involved in creation, and was active in the Old Testament, in the life of Christ, and in the lives of the apostles. In our last lesson we looked at how the Holy Spirit helps one become a Christian. However, for a Christian, a study of the Holy Spirit is not just a study of things that happened in the past.

The Holy Spirit is said to sanctify the child of God (Rom. 15:16; 2 Thess. 2:13; 1 Pet. 1:2). Sanctification has to do with purifying something and setting it aside for a special purpose. Paul described this when He taught that Jesus has sanctified and cleansed His church with the "washing of water by the word, that He might present her to Himself a glorious church, not having spot or wrinkle or any such thing, but that she should be holy and without blemish" (Eph. 5:26-27).

Christians have a special role to play in their service unto God. The Holy Spirit is given to the Christian so he can be equipped to serve in this role here on earth and then enjoy Heaven as his eternal home. In this lesson we will consider some important things the Holy Spirit does for the Christian today.

The Holy Spirit Leads the Christian

"For as many as are led by the Spirit of God, these are sons of God" (Rom. 8:14).

There is no doubt the faithful Christian is led by the Holy Spirit. The question is "How does the Holy Spirit lead us?" Some people today attribute their personal thoughts and decisions to the miraculous leading of the Holy Spirit. I have even heard some go so far as to credit the Holy Spirit with leading them to a good parking place at the shopping mall. To do so trivializes a great blessing from God. The Holy Spirit does not miraculously guide us through the daily decisions of our life. He leads us through the teaching found in His word.

The religious world is filled with people and churches that have different and conflicting beliefs and practices. Ironically, these people all claim to be led by the same Spirit. How is this possible? Jesus prayed that believers would be one (John 17:20-21). The apostle Paul pled with the church in Corinth, "that you all speak the same thing, and that there be no divisions among you, but that you be perfectly joined together in the same mind and in the same judgment" (1 Cor. 1:10). He also told them he taught the same thing in every church (4:17). The apostle John warned, "Beloved, do not believe every spirit, but test the spirits, whether they are of God; because many false prophets have gone out into the world" (1 John 4:1). The standard by which these spirits (teachers) were to be judged was that "which you heard from the beginning" (2:24)—the word of God. The division in the religious world invalidates the claim that these people are being led by the Holy Spirit.

The leading of the Holy Spirit is not against our will. Earlier in Romans chapter eight, Paul said, "For those who live according to the flesh set their minds on the things of the flesh, but those who live according to the Spirit, the things of the Spirit" (v. 5). Man is responsible for setting his mind upon the things of the Spirit. If his focus is upon the things of the Holy Spirit, he will be inclined to seek after and receive the leading of the Holy Spirit. As we have seen in a previous lesson, the Holy Spirit leads by spoken instruction, not by feelings or emotions.

As we have pointed out in our study, the Holy Spirit works through His word. This does no insult to the Holy Spirit, for He wrote the word. To be "filled with the Spirit" (Eph. 5:18) is to "let the word of Christ dwell in you richly" (Col. 3:16). We are sanctified by the Holy Spirit (2 Thess. 2:13), yet Jesus prayed that the Father would sanctify His disciples through His word (John 17:17). These two passages are speaking of the same thing—the Holy Spirit uses the word to accomplish the work of sanctification.

> Sanctify them by Your truth. Your word is truth.
>
> - John 17:17

One who is responding positively to the leading or guiding of the Holy Spirit will manifest a change in his conduct. He will allow the teaching of the Holy Spirit to produce a change in the way he thinks and lives. He will not fulfill the lust of the flesh (Gal. 5:16), but will bear the fruit of the Spirit (Gal. 5:22-23). The teachings of the Holy Spirit, as found in His word, will bring forth these changes in the life of a Christian.

The Holy Spirit Bears Witness With the Christian

"The Spirit Himself bears witness with our spirit that we are children of God" (Rom. 8:16).

The Holy Spirit does not abandon the Christian at the moment of his conversion. He continues to abide with the Christian and to bear witness to the fact that he is indeed a child of God. This work of the Holy Spirit is done in the spiritual realm and is not seen by the Christian in this world.

Satan is the accuser of God's people. He calls our faithfulness and our identity as a child of God into doubt (Job 1:9-11, 2:3-6; Zech. 3:1; Rev. 12:9-10). The Holy Spirit helps us refute such accusations. He bears witness with our spirit that we are a child of God. The Holy Spirit has set forth the conditions of salvation in His word. Our spirit knows whether or not we have truly met these conditions. When our spirit bears witness that we have met the conditions set forth by the Holy Spirit, there can be no doubt that we are saved. This gives us confidence as we face times of struggle and doubt.

The Holy Spirit has been given to the Christian as a seal and an earnest or guarantee (see 2 Cor. 1:21-22; Eph. 1:13-14).

Seal: the word "seal" has a number of different uses. In these passages, the word "seal" refers to a mark used to proclaim ownership. When we are saved, God uses the Holy Spirit to mark or identify us as His child (2 Tim. 2:19; Rev. 7:3). Although we cannot see this identifying mark in the physical realm, we benefit from knowing we do not escape God's notice or His protective care.

Earnest or Guarantee: an earnest is a pledge that is made for the purpose of giving assurance to another party. When one buys a home, he has to put down earnest money. The purpose of this payment is to assure the seller that you are serious and that you plan to follow through on your intention to buy their property. The Holy Spirit is given by God as "the guarantee of our inheritance" of Heaven (Eph. 1:14). The fact that God has given us the Holy Spirit to help us develop as Christians is assurance that He intends to follow through on His promise of Heaven. This assurance brings great comfort to every Christian.

The Holy Spirit Helps the Christian With His Prayers

"Likewise the Spirit also helps in our weaknesses. For we do not know what we should pray for as we ought, but the Spirit Himself makes intercession for us with groanings which cannot be uttered. Now He who searches the hearts knows what the mind of the Spirit is, because He makes intercession for the saints according to the will of God" (Rom. 8:26-27).

Christians can pray effectively (James 5:16), and the Bible teaches us the kinds of things for which we should be praying. However, situations arise in our life in which we have needs, longings, and pains that cannot adequately be expressed in words. These are times when we need God's

> Now He who establishes us with you in Christ and has anointed us is God, who also has sealed us and given us the Spirit in our hearts as a guarantee.
>
> - 2 Cor. 1:21-22

help, reach out to Him in prayer, but truly do not know exactly what to pray for. It is at times like this that the Holy Spirit intercedes for us.

To intercede is to seek one's presence on behalf of another. When the Holy Spirit makes intercession for us, He does not give us the words to say to God, but takes our inexpressible needs before God on our behalf. The barrier under consideration in this passage is our inability to express our needs. The Holy Spirit expresses these needs unto God. God, who knows the heart of man (Acts 1:24) and the mind of the Spirit, is then able to bless us according to our needs. This promise gives us great comfort during times of doubt, struggle, and grief.

The Holy Spirit Strengthens the Christian

"That He would grant you, according to the riches of His glory, to be strengthened with might through His Spirit in the inner man" (Eph. 3:16).

The Holy Spirit strengthens the heart or the spirit of man, but He does so through His word. It is the word of God that is able to build us up and strengthen us (Acts 20:32).

Paul prayed that the Colossians would be "strengthened with all might, according to His glorious power, for all patience and longsuffering with joy" (Col. 1:11). This strength was to come from a working knowledge of God's word. Paul specifically prayed, "that you may be filled with the knowledge of His will in all wisdom and spiritual understanding," and that they would be "increasing in the knowledge of God" (vs. 9-10). This knowledge of God's will, found in the word of God, would cause them to be "strengthened with all might, according to His glorious power."

The whole armor of God is given so the Christian can be strong in the Lord and stand against the attacks of the devil (Eph. 6:10-17). The crowning piece of this armor is the "sword of the Spirit, which is the word of God" (Eph. 6:17).

The strength given by the Holy Spirit through His word fortifies our faith and gives us the ability to patiently wait for the realization of our hope. "For we through the Spirit eagerly wait for the hope of righteousness by faith" (Gal. 5:5).

Conclusion

The Holy Spirit is not only interested in our initial conversion, but He is also interested in our development and steadfast faithfulness. He is given to us as an earnest or guarantee of our home in Heaven. He testifies to our identity as a child of God. Through His word, He strengthens us, guides us, and helps us make the necessary changes in our life. Finally, he helps us with our prayers so that we can continue to receive forgiveness and help from the Father.

Although much of His work goes unseen by mortal man, the Holy Spirit is very active in the life of the faithful Christian. However, we must make sure we do not attribute more activity to Him than what is actually revealed in the Word of God.

Questions

1. What does it mean to be sanctified? _____
_____

2. How is it possible for us to be sanctified by both the word of God (John 17:17) and the Holy Spirit (2 Thess. 2:13)? _____
_____

3. How does the Holy Spirit lead the Christian? _____
_____

4. What does Satan do to the child of God (Rev. 12:9-10)? _____
_____

5. How does the Holy Spirit bear witness with our spirit that we are children of God?
_____
_____

6. How is the Holy Spirit a seal to the Christian (2 Cor. 1:21-22; Eph. 1:13-14; Rev. 7:3)?
_____

7. What is an "earnest" or "guarantee," and how does the Holy Spirit fill this role for a Christian (2 Cor. 1:21-22; Eph. 1:13-14)? _____
_____

8. What is the Holy Spirit doing when He makes intercession for the child of God (Rom. 8:26-27)? _____
_____

9. What makes this intercession necessary? _____
_____

10. How does the Holy Spirit strengthen the Christian (Acts 20:32; Col. 1:9-11)? _____
_____

11. What is the "sword of the Spirit" (Eph. 6:17)? _____

The Indwelling of the Holy Spirit

The denominational world is filled with the teaching and conviction that the Holy Spirit personally and literally dwells within the Christian. Some claim this indwelling gives them special benefits such a better understanding of God's word and miraculous guidance in their daily life. Some of these claims become outrageous with people insisting the Holy Spirit keeps them from sinning or unleashes divine power in their life.

However, the belief in a literal, personal indwelling of the Holy Spirit is not limited to people in denominations. Although they may not make the same claims as mentioned above, some brethren believe in a literal indwelling of the Holy Spirit. This view is held by some who are sincere and very knowledgeable in the Scriptures, but it is a view which I believe to be contrary to the Scriptures.

There are some things about the Holy Spirit that are difficult to understand. The question of the indwelling is one of these difficult aspects of the Holy Spirit. It is not easy to understand the workings of deity and the spiritual world while we are confined to a physical existence. Although some things regarding the Holy Spirit are difficult, we must base our understandings of these things upon the teachings of the word of God, not upon feelings, opinions, desires, or denominational doctrines.

The Holy Spirit Dwells in the Christian

The Bible plainly says the Holy Spirit dwells in the Christian.

- "But you are not in the flesh but in the Spirit, if indeed the Spirit of God dwells in you. Now if anyone does not have the Spirit of Christ, he is not His... But if the Spirit of Him who raised Jesus from the dead dwells in you, He who raised Christ from the dead will also give life to your mortal bodies through His Spirit who dwells in you" (Romans 8:9, 11).

> Although some things regarding the Holy Spirit are difficult, we must base our understandings of these things upon the teachings of the word of God, not upon feelings, opinions, desires, or denominational doctrines.

- "Or do you not know that your body is the temple of the Holy Spirit who is in you, whom you have from God, and you are not your own?" (1 Corinthians 6:19).

- "That good thing which was committed to you, keep by the Holy Spirit who dwells in us" (2 Timothy 1:14).

- "Or do you think that the Scripture says in vain, 'The Spirit who dwells in us yearns jealously'" (James 4:5).

There is no doubt the Holy Spirit dwells in the Christian, but these verses are not proof texts for a personal, literal indwelling. Not one of these verses tells us how the Spirit dwells in us.

These verses are to be understood symbolically, not literally. As such, they emphasize the blessings that Christians enjoy with regards to having fellowship with the Holy Spirit as well as being influenced by the Holy Spirit.

Fellowship

...If we love one another, God abides in us...

- 1 Jn. 4:12

...that Christ may dwell in your hearts through faith...

- Eph. 3:17

The Bible says the Holy Spirit dwells in the Christian. However, the Bible also says both the Father and the Son dwell in the Christian (1 John 4:12-16, Eph. 3:17). Why is it that people want to emphasize the indwelling of the Holy Spirit, but not that of the Father and the Son? The Bible also says the Christian dwells in the Father (1 John 4:12-16), in the Son (John 6:56), and in the Holy Spirit (Gal. 5:25).

Fellowship With Deity

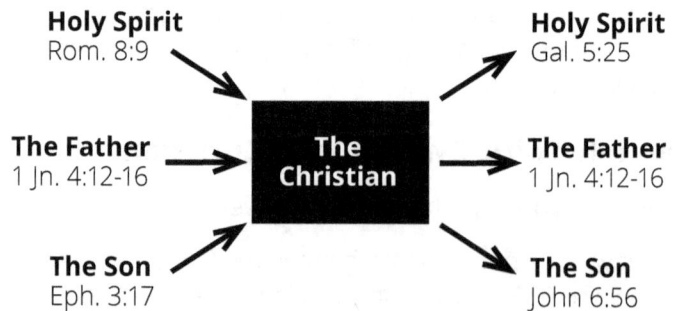

Holy Spirit
Rom. 8:9

The Father
1 Jn. 4:12-16

The Son
Eph. 3:17

The Christian

Holy Spirit
Gal. 5:25

The Father
1 Jn. 4:12-16

The Son
John 6:56

One of the rules of Bible study is that a passage is to be taken literally unless there is reason to take it figuratively. This teaching is confusing if we take it literally. How can a person dwell in a person who is dwelling within him? This does not make sense literally, but it makes perfect sense if taken figuratively. The figure of deity dwelling in us while we are dwelling in deity emphasizes the closeness of the fellowship we are to have with the Godhead (John 14:19-24). This fellowship is so close that each one is described as dwelling in the other.

Influence

One way a person can be said to "dwell in" another is to the extent that he can exert an influence over that person. For example, when a man is seen using the same mannerisms or figures of speech used by his father, an observer might say, "I can see your father in you." This is not understood literally, but figuratively. The observer sees the influence that the man's father has had on his life. The Holy Spirit can be seen in those who show the influence of the Holy Spirit in their lives; that is, they are living in the way the Holy Spirit tells them to live.

In Acts chapter four, Peter and John were arrested and later brought before the Sanhedrin. When these two apostles responded to the Jewish leaders in a bold manner, they realized Peter and John had been with Jesus (v. 13). They recognized the influence Jesus had upon their lives. Likewise, when the Bible speaks of the Holy Spirit dwelling in the Christian, it is, in part, emphasizing the influence that the Holy Spirit has upon our lives.

The Spirit and the Word

As we have already noted in our study, there is a connection between the Holy Spirit and the word of God. As we read and study the word of God, the Spirit has an **influence** upon our lives because the Spirit revealed the word unto mankind (1 Cor. 2:10-12, 2 Pet. 1:21). As we abide in the word, we maintain our **fellowship** with God (John 14:21, 23).

We considered a number of passages at the beginning of this lesson (Rom. 8:9, 11; 1 Cor. 6:19; 2 Tim. 1:14; James 4:5) which tell us the Holy Spirit dwells in us, but none of these passages tell us how the Holy Spirit comes to dwell in us. A miraculous, literal, personal indwelling has to be assumed. However, if we will continue to study the Scriptures, we will see there are passages which state how deity comes to dwell in the Christian.

- Christ is said to dwell in our hearts "through faith" (Eph. 3:17).

- The Galatians received the Holy Spirit "by the hearing of faith" (Gal. 3:2-5).

At that day you will know that I am in My Father, and you in Me, and I in you. He who has My commandments and keeps them, it is he who loves Me. And he who loves Me will be loved by My Father, and I will love him and manifest Myself to him."

- John 14:20-21

- Faith comes by hearing the word of God, not by a miraculous work of the Holy Spirit (Rom. 10:17).

Perhaps this connection between the indwelling of the Holy Spirit and the word of God is best seen in a comparison of two passages of Scripture.

The Holy Spirit and the Word of God

And do not be drunk with wine, in which is dissipation; but **be filled with the Spirit**, speaking to one another in psalms and hymns and spiritual songs, singing and making melody in your heart to the Lord.

Ephesians 5:18-19

Let the word of Christ dwell in you richly in all wisdom, teaching and admonishing one another in psalms and hymns and spiritual songs, singing with grace in your hearts to the Lord.

Colossians 3:16

The Bible is its own best commentary. When we set these two passages side by side we see that to be "filled with the Spirit" (Eph. 5:18) is the same as letting "the word of Christ dwell in" us richly (Col. 3:16). The Holy Spirit dwells in the Christian through the agency of the word of God. The blessings of this indwelling (fellowship with and influence from the Holy Spirit) are strengthened as we continue to read and abide in the word of God.

Consequences of a Literal, Personal Indwelling

The belief that the Holy Spirit personally, literally dwells in the Christian is not just a harmless opinion. There are some serious consequences to this view that must be considered.

1. **The written word becomes insufficient:** If a Christian can receive the blessings given in the word of God through some means independent and apart from the word, then the word is no longer necessary. If the indwelling of the Holy Spirit gives us guidance in our life, then we have all we need. While it would appear no one would want to accept this conclusion, it actually plays into the hands of those who 1) prefer emotionalism over reason and logic, and 2) are lazy and do not want to study the Bible.

2. **A dangerous step towards emotionalism and the charismatic movement:** Strange views are held by those in the denominational world regarding the literal indwelling of the Holy Spirit. Some of them believe they receive extra-biblical guidance and wisdom. They confuse the trained conscience with the speaking of the Spirit ("The Spirit laid this on my heart", etc.). Some of them insist it is impossible for them to sin because the Spirit dwelling in them would not allow them to sin. Brethren are falling into this kind of thinking, and the plain teaching of the Bible is being abandoned in favor of personal feelings and denominational error.

3. **The age of miracles has not ended:** God works in this world today through His providence. Any time deity interacts with this physical world in a direct way it is a miracle. For a member of the Godhead to literally and personally dwell in my physical body requires a miracle.

4. **We are Emmanuel:** What made Jesus different than any other man was the fact that deity dwelt in His physical body (Matt. 1:23). If the Holy Spirit literally dwells in me, why wouldn't I also be Immanuel? If the Father, Son, and Holy Spirit dwell directly and literally within my body, then why wouldn't I be the "fullness of the Godhead bodily" (Col. 2:9)? No serious Christian would ever make this kind of a claim, but this is what the literal indwelling of the Holy Spirit would make us.

Conclusion

The indwelling of the Holy Spirit is not an easy subject to understand, but we can understand what has been revealed about this subject. No one should deny that the Holy Spirit dwells in the Christian. The Bible teaches the Holy Spirit dwells in us through our faith and acceptance of His word. As we abide in His word, the Holy Spirit exerts an influence upon our lives and we enjoy fellowship with Him.

Questions

1. According to 1 Corinthians 6:19, what is a Christian's body? _____

    _____

2. According to passages like Romans 8:9, 2 Timothy 1:14, and James 4:5, what does the Holy Spirit do? _____

    _____

    _____

3. According to Ephesians 3:17, what does Jesus do? _____

    _____

    _____

4. According to 1 John 4:12-16, what does God the Father do? _____

    _____

    _____

5. According to passages like 1 John 4:12-16, John 6:56, and Galatians 5:25, what does the Christian do with all three members of the Godhead? _____

    _____

6. Is this mutual indwelling best understood in a literal, physical way or in a symbolic way? Why?_____

_____

_____

7. How is the Holy Spirit able to influence us through the word of God?_____

_____

_____

8. How does Christ come to dwell in our hearts (Eph. 3:17)? _____

_____

_____

9. How did the Galatians receive the Holy Spirit (Gal. 3:2-5; Rom. 10:17)?_____

_____

_____

10. How does a comparison of Ephesians 5:18-19 and Colossians 3:16 describe how a Christian is filled with the Holy Spirit?_____

_____

_____

11. What are some consequences of the literal, physical indwelling position? _____

_____

_____

_____

The Baptism of the Holy Spirit

Some people today believe they have the ability to speak in tongues, perform miracles of healing, and receive divine guidance in the affairs of their daily life. All of this is possible because they claim to have been baptized in the Holy Spirit.

Those who claim to receive Holy Spirit baptism are surprisingly divided over the purpose and timing of this baptism. For instance, the United Pentecostal Church believes Holy Spirit baptism is a part of the "new birth" (being born of the water and the Spirit—John 3:5). They teach one cannot be saved until he has been baptized in the Holy Spirit and in water. The Assembly of God Church teaches the baptism of the Holy Spirit is a "second work of grace" that comes after salvation, equipping the believer to live a more fulfilling life in service unto God.

Those who see Holy Spirit baptism as a "second work of grace" believe it is the means of a Christian moving on to a higher level of spiritual life. As some have put it, without Holy Spirit baptism, "you cannot function the way God really wants you to. You are missing something. You are an eight cylinder engine firing on four, or possibly six at the most. You are just not quite there" (MacArthur 249). As such, Holy Spirit baptism is something that is earnestly sought after by these individuals:

> "Charismatics generally believe that after someone becomes a Christian, he or she must seek diligently for the baptism of the Spirit. Those who get this baptism also experience various phenomena, such as speaking in tongues, feelings of euphoria, visions, and emotional outbursts of various kinds. Those who have not experienced the baptism and its accompanying phenomena are not considered Spirit-filled; that is, they are immature, carnal, disobedient, or otherwise incomplete Christians" (ibid, p. 27).

> "Pentecostals declare that what many Christians today need is precisely this baptism of power. In addition to being born of the Spirit wherein new life

> Those who claim to receive Holy Spirit baptism are surprisingly divided over the purpose and timing of this baptism.

Buried with Him in baptism, in which you also were raised with Him through faith in the working of God, who raised Him from the dead.

- Col. 2:12

begins, there is also the need for being baptized, or filled, with the Spirit for the outflow of the life in ministry to others" (Burgess, McGee, Alexander 46).

These types of claims are becoming more common today. The "Community Church" movement has removed barriers between those in various denominations, and now these false beliefs regarding the baptism of the Holy Spirit are heard from all across the religious landscape. Unfortunately, a lack of teaching has left brethren unequipped to address this error. In this lesson we will consider who this baptism was for and the purpose it was intended to serve.

Jesus is the Administrator of Holy Spirit Baptism

The word "baptism" is translated from the Greek word *baptisma* which means to be immersed. The New Testament likens baptism to a burial (Rom. 6:3-4, Col. 2:12). To undergo the baptism of the Holy Spirit means to be immersed in the Holy Spirit. The Holy Spirit is not the administrator (the one who does the baptizing). He is the element (that in which one is baptized).

Jesus is the one who administers the baptism of the Holy Spirit. The baptism of the Holy Spirit is first mentioned by John the Baptist. "I did not know Him, but He who sent me to baptize with water said to me, 'Upon whom you see the Spirit descending, and remaining on Him, this is He who baptizes with the Holy Spirit'" (John 1:33). John proclaimed that Jesus would baptize with the Holy Spirit. "I indeed baptize you with water unto repentance, but He who is coming after me is mightier than I, whose sandals I am not worthy to carry. He will baptize you with the Holy Spirit and fire" (Matt. 3:11). This baptism took place in Acts chapter two (verses 1-4). When questioned about the events surrounding this baptism, Peter said it was Jesus who had poured forth what they were seeing and hearing (vv. 32-33).

The Baptism of the Holy Spirit Was A Promise

The New Testament teaches the baptism of the Holy Spirit was a promise, not a command. This is an important distinction; promises are to be received and enjoyed, while commands are to be obeyed.

"And being assembled together with them, He commanded them not to depart from Jerusalem, but to wait for the **Promise** of the Father, 'which,' He said, 'you have heard from Me; for John truly baptized with water, but **you shall be baptized with the Holy Spirit** not many days from now... But you shall receive power **when the Holy Spirit has come upon you**; and you shall be witnesses to Me in Jerusalem, and in all Judea and Samaria, and to the end of the earth'" (Acts 1:4-5, 8; emphasis mine—HR).

Water baptism is a command of the Lord to be obeyed (Mark 16:16; Acts 10:48, 22:16). No one ever obeyed a command to be baptized in the Holy Spirit. Individuals simply received this baptism from the Lord.

This Promise Was For the Apostles

The promise of the baptism of the Holy Spirit was made to the apostles, not all of mankind. This promise was made in Luke 24:44-49 and Acts 1:4-8. In both passages, Jesus was talking with the apostles, not to all His followers. He told them to wait in Jerusalem for the promise of the Father, which is the baptism of the Holy Spirit. This baptism would give them power and equip them to do the work of an apostle; to bear witness of His resurrection and to preach the gospel in His name to all nations.

In lesson five, we took note of the special relationship between the Holy Spirit and the apostles. They would enjoy a measure of the Holy Spirit not promised to all men which would equip them to do their work. This power or measure of the Spirit was given to them in Acts chapter two when they were baptized in the Holy Spirit by Jesus Christ. No one else ever received the Holy Spirit in this measure.

Objections

Those who believe they have received the baptism of the Holy Spirit will object to the teaching that this baptism was limited to the apostles. The following are some of the objections that have been offered.

1. **All of the believers received the outpouring of the Holy Spirit in Acts 2.** Acts 1:15 says there were about 120 disciples in Jerusalem during that time. The argument is made that the Holy Spirit did not just fall upon the twelve apostles, but upon all these disciples.

> No one ever obeyed a command to be baptized in the Holy Spirit. Individuals simply received this baptism from the Lord.

This objection is answered by looking at the account of the baptism of the Holy Spirit in Acts 2:1-4.

1   When the Day of Pentecost had fully come, **they** were all with one accord in one place.

2   And suddenly there came a sound from heaven, as of a rushing mighty wind, and it filled the whole house where **they** were sitting.

3   Then there appeared to **them** divided tongues, as of fire, and one sat upon each of **them**.

4   And **they** were all filled with the Holy Spirit and began to speak with other tongues, as the Spirit gave **them** utterance (emphasis mine—HR).

The text does not specify the individuals by name or by number. It simply says "they" and "them." Who are the "they" and "them?" If one looks at the pervious verse (remembering the chapter and verse divisions have been added by man) he will learn the identity of the "they" and "them." "And they cast their lots, and the lot fell on Matthias. And he was numbered with the eleven **apostles**" (Acts 1:26; emphasis mine—HR). Who were the recipients of the baptism of the Holy Spirit? It was the apostles, not all the disciples.

2. **John taught that Jesus would baptize all men with the Holy Spirit.** "I indeed baptize you with water unto repentance, but He who is coming after me is mightier than I, whose sandals I am not worthy to carry. He will baptize you with the Holy Spirit and fire" (Matt. 3:11).

John was not promising that everyone would receive the baptism of the Holy Spirit. John did not even baptize everyone with water (vv. 7-10). John was emphasizing the fact that Jesus was mightier than himself. While John baptized men with water unto repentance, Jesus had the ability to baptize men with the Holy Spirit and with fire. The baptism of fire is not Holy Spirit baptism. Verse twelve indicates this baptism is the right and ability to cast one into Hell. Hell is an immersion in fire (Rev. 20:14-15). John was not promising that everyone present would receive the baptism of the Holy Spirit and the baptism of fire, he was talking about the baptisms that Jesus had the power to administer. Some men would be baptized by Jesus with the Holy Spirit and some would

Who were the recipients of the baptism of the Holy Spirit? It was the apostles, not all the disciples.

be baptized with fire. We learn from other passages (like Luke 24:44-49 and Acts 1:4-8) that the baptism of the Holy Spirit was intended for the apostles.

3. **The prophecy of Joel quoted by Peter in Acts 2 says the Holy Spirit would be poured out "on all flesh" (vv. 17-18), thus, all believers are to receive the baptism of the Holy Spirit.** The text reads, "And it shall come to pass in the last days, says God, that I will pour out of My Spirit on all flesh; your sons and your daughters shall prophesy, your young men shall see visions, your old men shall dream dreams. And on My menservants and on My maidservants I will pour out My Spirit in those days; and they shall prophesy."

This passage from Joel is quoted by Peter as an explanation of the amazing things those in the crowd were witnessing (Acts 2:5-13). The baptism of the Holy Spirit upon the apostles was a fulfillment of this prophecy of Joel. Only the apostles were baptized in the Holy Spirit, but the baptism of the Holy Spirit empowered the apostles to perform a work that would benefit "all flesh" (men and women, young and old, Jew and eventually Gentile). Some believers received the miraculous gifts of the Holy Spirit in a limited measure (prophesying, seeing visions and dreams, etc.) through the laying on of the hands of an apostles (Acts 8:18). "All flesh" received the gospel message inspired by the Holy Spirit through the preaching of the apostles, extending the invitation "that whoever calls on the name of the Lord shall be saved" (Acts 2:21).

What About the Household of Cornelius?

Those at the household of Cornelius experienced a baptism of the Holy Spirit (Acts 10:44-48). Does this prove such was a common occurrence in the First Century and, thus, should be expected to happen every time a person is saved today?

The baptism of the Holy Spirit that occurred on Pentecost (Acts 2) equipped the apostles, but it was also a sign to the unbelievers. It attracted their attention (v. 6) and gave credibility to the message that was preached by the apostles (v. 33).

The baptism of the Holy Spirit that occurred at the household of Cornelius was also a sign, but the unbelievers

While Peter was still speaking these words, the Holy Spirit fell upon all those who heard the word. And those of the circumcision who believed were astonished, as many as came with Peter, because the gift of the Holy Spirit had been poured out on the Gentiles also.

- Acts 10:44-45

in this case were Peter and the six Jewish Christians who were with him. Notice three things Peter did when the Holy Spirit fell upon these Gentiles. First, he recognized it as that which had happened to the apostles on Pentecost (11:15). Second, he identified it as Holy Spirit baptism (11:16). Third, he immediately concluded these Gentiles were appropriate candidates for baptism (10:47-48, 11:17). It was a special occurrence for a special purpose, unique to this account of conversion. It was just one of several extraordinary things God did to get Peter and the rest of the Jewish Christians to understand the Gentiles were to receive the gospel.

Conclusion

As was quoted in the lesson, some people believe those who have not received Holy Spirit baptism are "immature, carnal, disobedient, or otherwise incomplete Christians." Because of this, believers are encouraged to "seek diligently for the baptism of the Spirit." However, no apostle ever encouraged Christians to be baptized in the Holy Spirit. We are told that without Holy Spirit baptism "you cannot function the way God really wants you to," but Paul said all Scripture was the means by which "the man of God may be complete, thoroughly equipped for every good work" (2 Tim. 3:17). If all Scripture makes me thoroughly equipped for every good work, what need do I have for the baptism of the Holy Spirit?

Holy Spirit baptism was not a command to be obeyed. It was a limited promise which served its purpose. The apostles were empowered to do their work when they were baptized with the Holy Spirit, and we can benefit from the work the Holy Spirit did through the apostles when we study the New Testament, but the promise of the baptism of the Holy Spirit is not for us.

References

Burgess, Stanley M., McGee, Gary B., Alexander, Patrick H. *Dictionary of Pentecostal and Charismatic Movements*. Grand Rapids, MI. Regency Reference Library, 1988. Print.

MacArthur, Jr., John F. *Charismatic Chaos*. Grand Rapids, MI: Zondervan Publishing House, 1992. Print.

Questions

1. What does the word "baptism" mean? _____

    _____

2. What is baptism likened unto in Romans 6:3-4 and Colossians 2:12?_____

    _____

3. Who administers (performs) the baptism of the Holy Spirit (John 1:33) _____

    _____

4. Is the baptism of the Holy Spirit a promise or a command? _____

5. Why did the apostles receive the baptism of the Holy Spirit (Luke 24:44-49; Acts 1:4-8)?_____

    _____

6. How do we know that only the apostles were baptized with the Holy Spirit in Acts 2:1-4? _____

    _____

    _____

7. Is the baptism of the Holy Spirit and the baptism of fire the same thing (Matt. 3:11-12)? Why or why not? _____

    _____

    _____

8. Describe what happened when the apostles were baptized in the Holy Spirit (Acts 2:1-4). _____

    _____

9. Describe what happened when the Holy Spirit fell upon the household of Cornelius (Acts 10:44-48)._____

    _____

10. What event did Peter liken this unto (Acts 11:15-16)?_____

    _____

11. Why did the Holy Spirit fall upon the household of Cornelius (Acts 10:47, 11:17-18)?

    _____

    _____

12. Does the Bible teach that the Holy Spirit fell upon everyone who was converted to Christ, or was what happened at the house of Cornelius a special, one-time event?

    _____

    _____

The Miraculous Gifts of the Holy Spirit

The church in Corinth needed help in many areas. Among their problems was a misunderstanding and misuse of the miraculous gifts of the Holy Spirit. Paul addressed this problem in First Corinthians chapters 12-14. In the midst of these instructions, Paul gave the following list of these gifts.

> For to one is given the word of wisdom through the Spirit, to another the word of knowledge through the same Spirit, to another faith by the same Spirit, to another gifts of healings by the same Spirit, to another the working of miracles, to another prophecy, to another discerning of spirits, to another different kinds of tongues, to another the interpretation of tongues (1 Corinthians 12:8-10).

The above passage is not meant to be an exhaustive list of the miraculous gifts of the Holy Spirit, but many of them are included. We cannot deny the fact these gifts existed and served an important purpose in the early church. However, there are many people today who believe these gifts still exist. These people claim they have the ability to do things like speak in tongues, prophecy, or work miracles. There was a time when these claims were limited to members of charismatic or holiness churches, but these beliefs can now be found among members of mainstream denominations as well as some in the Catholic Church.

It is generally hard to reason with these people. No one doubts their sincerity, but they usually rely upon their feelings and would rather "testify" about their experiences than study what the Bible says. Some are even heard to say, "I would rather have what I feel in my heart than a whole stack of Bibles," while the Bible says, "The heart is deceitful above all things, and desperately wicked; who can know it?" (Jer. 17:9).

The question is not, "Have these people witnessed or experienced something?" They believe they have, and it would be futile for us to try to tell them they haven't. The real question is, "What does the Bible say about the miraculous gifts of the Holy Spirit?" In particular, does the

No one doubts their sincerity, but they usually rely upon their feelings and would rather "testify" about their experiences than study what the Bible says.

The Gift of Healing

One might make a case that the gift of healing satisfies a non-spiritual need. However, a close study of the New Testament will show the gift of healing was not primarily for the physical benefit of the one being healed. It was a sign which confirmed the word.

Paul told the Philippians that Epaphroditus was "sick almost unto death" (Phil. 2:25-30). Why didn't Paul heal him of this sickness? Because there was no spiritual need—both men were believers. In Second Corinthians we read about Paul praying for relief from his thorn in the flesh (2 Cor. 12:7-10). Why didn't some Christian heal Paul of this physical malady? Because Paul was already a believer, and the thorn in the flesh was actually needed to keep him humble.

These gifts, even the gift of healing, were signs to confirm the word. The word has already been confirmed, so all of these gifts have served their purpose.

Bible teach these gifts were meant for believers of all time or have they served their purpose and ceased to exist?

The Purpose For the Miraculous Gifts of the Holy Spirit

God has a reason for everything He does. If we can understand the reason for the miraculous gifts of the Holy Spirit, we can better understand and appreciate their intended duration.

1. **Deliver the truth in the absence of completed revelation:** The First Century church did not have the New Testament as we have it today. These early saints relied upon miraculous gifts to receive God's word piece by piece (1 Cor. 14:26). Those who had the gift of wisdom, knowledge, prophecy, or tongues would deliver inspired revelations of God's word to the church when it was assembled. It was through these gifts that the early church received needed edification (1 Cor. 14:3, 12). In the absence of an apostle, local congregations needed these gifts in order to be established in the word (Rom. 1:11).

2. **Confirm the spoken word:** The word "confirm" means to certify or prove a thing is genuine or true. As the apostles and evangelists went out preaching the gospel, the miraculous gifts would accompany their preaching and prove it to be the true word of God (Mark 16:20).

"Then Philip went down to the city of Samaria and preached Christ to them. And the multitudes with one accord heeded the things spoken by Philip, hearing and seeing the miracles which he did" (Acts 8:5-6). The people of Samaria took Philip's message seriously when they saw the miracles he performed. If a stranger came to town talking about a man named Jesus who was crucified and had risen from the dead, his message would be mocked and rejected (Acts 17:32). However, if this stranger healed the sick and raised someone from the dead, the people would take his message seriously.

When God's revelation was completed and compiled into the New Testament, there ceased to be a need for revealing it and confirming it through the miraculous gifts of the Holy Spirit. The word has been delivered in its entirety (Jude 3) and sufficiently confirmed (Heb. 2:3-4). The gifts have served their purpose. Think about it:

what spiritual need is there that the revealed, confirmed word of God does not satisfy?

Means of Receiving the Miraculous Gifts of the Holy Spirit

According to the New Testament, the way one received the miraculous gifts of the Holy Spirit was through the laying on of the hands of an apostle.

- This was the reason the apostles Peter and John were sent to the new believers in Samaria, and this is exactly what Simon saw them doing (Acts 8:14-19).

- This is why Paul wanted to go to the church in Rome (Rom. 1:11).

- This is how Timothy received his spiritual gift (2 Tim. 1:6).

After the last apostle died, the means of receiving the miraculous gifts of the Holy Spirit were gone. In order for people to have these gifts today 1) an apostle is still alive, 2) some who received these gifts from an apostle are still alive, 3) God is now imparting these gifts to men in a different manner. All three possibilities must be rejected by honest Bible students.

The Duration of the Miraculous Gifts of the Holy Spirit

The New Testament tells us how long God intended these miraculous gifts to last. When Paul was addressing the subject of miraculous gifts with the church in Corinth he paused to talk about the superiority of love (1 Cor. 13). One of the things that made love superior to these gifts was that love would outlast all these gifts. Consider the following verses:

> Love never fails. But whether there are prophecies, they will fail; whether there are tongues, they will cease; whether there is knowledge, it will vanish away. For we know in part and we prophesy in part. But when that which is perfect has come, then that which is in part will be done away.
> (1 Corinthians 13:8-10).

According to Paul, the miraculous gifts (prophecies, tongues, miraculous knowledge) will "fail," "cease," and "vanish away." When will this happen? According to verse ten, these gifts will

> For I long to see you, that I may impart to you some spiritual gift, so that you may be established...
>
> - Rom. 1:11

vanish when "that which is perfect has come." What is that which is perfect? Some claim this is a reference to Christ, indicating these miraculous gifts were meant to last until the Second Coming of Christ. Christ certainly is "perfect," but this interpretation does not fit the passage. According to verse ten, the "perfect" has to correspond to the "part." The "parts" make up that which is "perfect." To know what the "perfect" is, we have to identify the "part."

Verse nine says "we know in part and we prophecy in part." Remember, the miraculous gifts were the means by which God revealed His will to the early church in the absence of the New Testament. When the saints assembled on the Lord's Day, those with the gifts did not recite the entire content of the New Testament at every assembly. They did what gospel preachers do today - they revealed a "part" of God's will.

According to Paul, the "perfect" would take the place of the "part." If the "part" was receiving God's revelation piece by piece, then the "perfect" is the entirety of God's revelation. The New Testament is the "perfect," complete revelation of God's will to mankind in this dispensation.

Consider what was happening in the early church. These gifts were given by the laying on of the hands of an apostle. When the last apostle died, no one else received these gifts. When the generation of Christians who had last received these gifts from the apostles died, these gifts vanished from the earth. At the same time, the writings of the apostles and other inspired men were being copied and transmitted among the churches. As those with the gifts were disappearing, the New Testament was taking form. By the time those with the gifts (the "part") left, the New Testament (the "perfect") was available. The gifts were no longer needed because the will of God had been revealed and confirmed. Thus, the New Testament does indeed address the duration of the miraculous gifts of the Holy Spirit. They disappeared from the earth a long time ago.

Continuing with the instructions in First Corinthians thirteen, Paul uses two illustrations to show the temporary nature of the miraculous gifts.

> When I was a child, I spoke as a child, I understood as a child, I thought as a child; but when I became a man, I put away childish things. For now we see in

Scaffolding is often employed when a building is under construction. The scaffolding is taken down when the construction is complete. The miraculous gifts helped the church in its infancy. After the church was fully established, and equipped with the complete revelation of the New Testament, the gifts were removed. They are no longer needed. Those who want to return to the age of miraculous gifts want to keep the scaffolding up. They prefer the church in its infancy rather than in its maturity.

a mirror, dimly, but then face to face. Now I know in part, but then I shall know just as I also am known (1 Corinthians 13:11-12).

Paul speaks of his transition from childhood into adulthood. We understand many things change as one makes this transition. There are things one needs as a baby and as a child that he does not need as an adult. The church in its infancy needed the miraculous gifts in order to be established (Rom. 1:11). When the church outgrew this stage, these gifts were no longer needed.

Paul also speaks of the difference between seeing his image dimly in a mirror and then seeing it clearly "face to face." Mirrors in the First Century were polished metal. They did not produce a clear reflection as our mirrors do today. One could look into a mirror and get an idea of one's appearance, but not the perfect or complete reflection of his appearance. Likewise, the miraculous gifts allowed the early Christians to catch a "piece by piece" glance of God's revelation, but the New Testament gives us the complete "picture" of God's will.

Conclusion

There is no doubt the miraculous gifts of the Holy Spirit existed and played an important role in the early church. However, a careful study of the New Testament indicates these gifts served their purpose and lasted for their intended duration.

The apostle Paul told the Corinthians a better day was coming when the "perfect" would do away with the "part." While some people today claim to be exercising these gifts (the part), we understand that we are actually living in that better day of which Paul spoke. We have the "perfect," complete revelation of God's will in the New Testament.

Questions

1. List the nine miraculous gifts mentioned in 1 Corinthians 12:8-10._____

_____

_____

2. Who gave these gifts to the Corinthians (vv. 8-9)?_____

_____

3. What did the gifts of wisdom, knowledge, prophecy, and tongues provide for the early church (1 Cor. 14:3, 12, 26)?_____

_____

4. What does the word "confirm" mean? _____

_____

5. Explain how the miraculous gifts of the Holy Spirit confirmed the word of God.

    _____

    _____

6. Has the word of God been revealed and confirmed (Jude 3; Heb. 1:3-4)?_____

7. How do we know the gift of healing was not primarily for the physical benefit of the individual who was healed (Phil. 2:25-30; 2 Cor. 12:7-10)? _____

    _____

8. How did Christians receive the miraculous gifts of the Holy Spirit (Acts 8:14-19; Rom. 1:11; 2 Tim. 1:6)?_____

    _____

9. According to your answer to the above question, is it possible for anyone to possess these gifts today? _____

10. What three miraculous gifts of the Holy Spirit are mentioned in 1 Corinthians 13:8, and what three words or phrases are used to indicate they will no longer be in use?

    _____

    _____

11. When will the knowing and prophesying "in part" be done away with (v. 10)?_____

    _____

12. If "the part" is receiving God's revelation piece-by-piece through the miraculous gifts of the Holy Spirit, what is "the perfect" (Remember, the "perfect" is the sum total of the "parts.")?_____

    _____

13. What two illustrations did Paul use to indicate the temporary nature of the miraculous gifts of the Holy Spirit (1 Cor. 13:11-12)? _____

    _____

14. Why don't we need these gifts today? _____

    _____

Speaking in Tongues

In our previous lesson, we studied the miraculous gifts of the Holy Spirit in general. In this lesson we will focus our study upon one particular gift—the gift of tongues.

The Corinthians were enamored with the gift of tongues (1 Cor. 14:1-25), but that should be of no surprise to us, for many religious people around us today are equally fascinated with speaking in tongues. There was a time when only those who were in holiness or charismatic churches claimed to possess the ability to speak in tongues, but today this claim is made by those who are in more mainstream denominations, community churches, and even by some in the Catholic church. This means we are more likely to come into contact with those who claim to exercise this gift, or others who have questions about speaking in tongues. We would do well to study this subject so we can be grounded in our own faith and be able to teach others.

What is the Gift of Tongues?

Perhaps no miraculous gift is better described in the New Testament than the gift of tongues.

In Acts chapter two, the Holy Spirit fell upon the apostles and they "began to speak with other tongues, as the Spirit gave them utterance" (v. 4). Being a feast day, Jerusalem was filled with Jews from many different nations. These Jews were amazed because they heard the apostles speaking in the languages of their home nations.

- "...everyone heard them speak in his own language" (v. 6).

- "And how is it that we hear, each in our own language in which we were born?" (v. 8).

- "...we hear them speaking in our own tongues the wonderful works of God" (v. 11).

This passage identifies what is meant by speaking with "new tongues" (Mark 16:17) or "other tongues" (Acts 2:4). The gift of tongues was the miraculous ability to speak in a known

And these signs will follow those who believe: In My name they will cast out demons; they will speak with new tongues...

- Mark 16:17

and recognizable language that one had never learned. This is not the practice of many who claim to have the gift of tongues today. While the Jews on Pentecost heard the apostles speak in recognizable foreign languages, "tongue speakers" today are heard to utter unintelligible sounds often called "ecstatic utterances." This practice does not follow the pattern set forth in the New Testament, and thus is not the gift of tongues that was given by the Holy Spirit.

Some modern day tongue speakers claim the unintelligible sounds made when they speak in tongues are not a human language, but are the "tongues of angels." In First Corinthians 13:1 Paul said, "Though I speak with the tongues of men and of angels, but have not love, I have become sounding brass or a clanging cymbal." Are these modern tongue speakers really speaking an angelic language which is unrecognizable to men?

To address this question, one needs to consider the context of First Corinthians chapter thirteen. Paul begins this chapter by making three hypothetical statements, purposefully exaggerated, to emphasize the superiority of love over miraculous gifts of the Holy Spirit (1 Cor. 12:31). He speaks of the ineffectiveness of the gift of tongues (v. 1), the ability to move mountains (v. 2), and the sacrificing of his physical body (v. 3) without the presence of love.

> But earnestly desire the best gifts. And yet I show you a more excellent way.
>
> - 1 Cor. 12:31

When Paul mentions speaking with the tongues of angels, we must remember the purpose of these verses. Paul was not affirming that he and others actually spoke the language of angels (or literally moved mountains or gave their bodies to be burned). He was saying the possession of such great abilities, without love, would be nothing.

Paul used angels in a similar way in Galatians 1:8. "But even if we, or an angel from heaven, preach any other gospel to you than what we have preached to you, let him be accursed." Angels did not preach the gospel to anyone. That responsibility was given to Christians. Paul's point is that even if a great being such as an angel were to preach a perverted gospel, he would be cursed and his message was not to be accepted.

Both uses of angels (1 Cor. 13:1; Gal. 1:8) should be understood figuratively, not literally. The gift of tongues was the miraculous ability to speak in a recognizable language that one had never learned.

The Purpose for the Gift of Tongues

There is a reason behind everything God does, including the spiritual gifts He bestowed upon men through His Spirit. The gift of tongues was a confirming sign for unbelievers. "Therefore tongues are for a sign, not to those who believe but to unbelievers..." (1 Cor. 14:22; cf. Mark 16:17-18, 20).

In our previous lesson, we learned that miraculous gifts of the Holy Spirit were given to confirm the word spoken by the apostles and other evangelists of the First Century. To confirm means to certify or prove that a thing is genuine or true. As the apostles preached, the gifts (such as speaking in tongues) served to certify or confirm the validity of their message.

In Acts chapter two, Jews from several different nations were assembled in Jerusalem for the feast of Pentecost. They were amazed and marveled when they heard the twelve Galileans speaking the languages of their home countries. They recognized this was a sign and asked what it could mean (vv. 11-12). Peter began to preach the gospel. He said Jesus, who had risen from the dead and was exalted to the right hand of God, had poured forth what they were seeing and hearing (vv. 32-33). Peter went on to identify Jesus as their "Lord and Christ." When asked what they should do, Peter told them to repent and be baptized in the name of Jesus Christ for the remission of their sins (vv. 36-38). About three thousand of these Jews obeyed Peter's word (v. 41). In this account, the gift of tongues served as a sign to the unbelieving Jews, convincing them that Jesus really was the Christ, and that they needed to repent and be baptized.

The next time we read of tongues is in Acts chapter ten. This is the account of the conversion of the household of Cornelius. Interestingly, it is not the apostle Peter or other Jewish Christians who spoke in tongues in this account. The Holy Spirit fell upon the Gentiles and they began to speak in tongues (vv. 44-46). This convinced Peter that the uncircumcised Gentiles were proper candidates for baptism. When questioned by Jewish Christians in Jerusalem, Peter defended his actions by pointing to the pouring out of the Holy Spirit and their speaking in tongues (Acts 11:15-18). Tongues were a sign on this occasion, but the "unbelievers" were Peter and the other Jewish Christians who had to be convinced that the gospel was for uncircumcised Gentiles as well as for Jews.

> And those of the circumcision who believed were astonished, as many as came with Peter, because the gift of the Holy Spirit had been poured out on the Gentiles also. For they heard them speak with tongues and magnify God.
>
> - Acts 10:44-45

The gift of tongues is also found in Acts chapter nineteen. Paul encountered twelve disciples when he returned to Ephesus. He asked them if they had received the Holy Spirit, to which they replied, "We have not so much as heard whether there is a Holy Spirit" (v. 2). Upon further questioning, Paul realized they only knew about the baptism of John. He taught them the gospel, baptized them in the name of the Lord Jesus, laid his hands upon them, and the Holy Spirit came upon them and they spoke with tongues (vv. 3-6). In this passage, the disciples were the unbelievers. Tongues were a sign assuring them they had done the right thing. It was God's will that the disciples of John the Baptist be baptized into Christ for the remission of their sins.

The other purpose for miraculous gifts of the Holy Spirit was to deliver God's word in the absence of completed revelation. In First Corinthians chapter fourteen, Paul addressed the church's misuse of the gift of tongues. He taught them the gift of tongues, like all other miraculous gifts, was to be used for the edification of the whole church, not for the glorification of the speaker (vv. 1-6, 12-13, 18-19, 26).

The possession of the gift of tongues was never an indication or proof of one's salvation or sanctification. Consider the following facts:

- Tongues are only mentioned with three accounts of conversion in the book of Acts.

- Those in Cornelius' household spoke in tongues prior to their baptism (before they were saved).

- All of the Corinthians were sanctified (1 Cor. 1:2), but not all of them spoke in tongues (12:10, 29-30; 14:3).

- The gift of tongues is only mentioned in one epistle of the New Testament (First Corinthians). If the gift of tongues was to play a permanent role in the life of every Christian, one would think the subject would have been addressed more often in the New Testament.

Bible Tongues vs. Modern Day Tongues

There are a number of contradictions between the modern practice of speaking in tongues and the gift of tongues that appears in the New Testament.

Are all apostles? Are all prophets? Are all teachers? Are all workers of miracles? Do all have gifts of healings? Do all speak with tongues? Do all interpret?

- 1 Cor. 12:29-30

1. **Tongues were a recognizable language.** In the Bible, the gift of tongues was the ability to speak in an existing language that the speaker did not know. Modern day tongue speaking is the utterance of unintelligible sounds which no one can recognize or understand.

   While the modern day practice of speaking in tongues differs from the pattern set forth in the New Testament, it is surprisingly close to practices found in other cultures—both modern and ancient. Linguist specialists have observed modern tongues speaking taking place among Muslims, Mormons, Eskimos, those who practice Voodoo, Buddhists, Tibetan monks, and Shinto priests. The "ecstatic utterances" produced by modern tongue speakers, and the emotional circumstances that often surround and lead to the practice, resemble the "ecstasy" that was/is experienced by those in the mystery or pagan religions of the world. The modern day tongue movement has not come from God. It is a learned behavior that is found in a great many non-Christian religions throughout the world and throughout history.

2. **People are taught how to speak in tongues.** That which passes for speaking in tongues in the modern day tongue movement is not a miraculous gift of the Holy Spirit; it is a learned behavior. Many charismatics claim to be able to teach others to speak in tongues. Some even hold seminars to instruct people how to receive the gift of tongues. Often times, people are told to repeat basic sounds over and over. People who earnestly desire this gift, and repeat these sounds over and over again in an emotionally charged charismatic worship service, can certainly talk themselves into thinking they have the gift of tongues.

   Think carefully, those who received the gift of tongues in the New Testament did not receive instructions from any man on how to receive or use this gift. They simply began speaking in tongues as the Holy Spirit gave them utterance. The modern day tongue movement is a fraud.

3. **The gift of tongues could be controlled.** "If anyone speaks in a tongue, let there be two or at the most three, each in turn, and let one interpret. But if there is no interpreter, let him keep silent in church, and let him speak to himself and to God" (1 Cor. 14:27-28).

> The modern day practice of speaking in tongues is a learned behavior that is found in a great many non-Christian religions throughout the world and throughout history.

The modern day tongues movement thrives in an atmosphere of excitement and purposeful lack of control.

4. **The gift of tongues ceased.** As we saw in the previous lesson, all miraculous gifts of the Holy Spirit served their purpose and vanished away (1 Cor. 13:8-12). Some modern day tongue speakers claim the gift never went away, while others claim it vanished but has revived. Both views are contrary to Scripture.

Conclusion

Just as was the case in Corinth, the gift of tongues is sought after and abused today. If one will set aside personal feelings and opinions, and honestly examine the teachings of the New Testament, he will find that the modern day practice of speaking in tongues is not the same as the gift given by the Holy Spirit and exercised by Christians in the New Testament.

The gift of tongues was the ability to speak in an existing human language that one had never learned. This gift was a sign to unbelievers and, if accompanied by an interpreter, was to be used to edify the church. Like all other miraculous gifts of the Holy Spirit, the gift of tongues vanished away and we are left with the complete revelation of God's will in the New Testament.

Questions

1. What was the gift of tongues (Acts 2:4, 6, 8, 11)? _____

   _____

2. What was the purpose for the gift of tongues (1 Cor. 14:22)? _____

   _____

3. Who were the "unbelievers" in Acts 2? _____

   _____

4. Who were the "unbelievers" in Acts 10? _____

   _____

5. Who were the "unbelievers" in Acts 19? _____

   _____

6. According to First Corinthians chapter fourteen, what purpose did the gift of tongues serve in the assemblies of the church (vv. 5, 12-13, 26)? _____

   _____

7. What was the tongue speaker to do if there was no one with the gift of interpretation present in the assembly (1 Cor. 14:28)? _____

Discussion Questions

1. Why should we study what the New Testament has to say about speaking in tongues?

2. Because the sounds they make are not a recognizable language, some modern tongue speakers claim their gift is the ability to speak the language of angels (1 Cor. 13:1). How would you respond to this claim?

3. Some people believe the gift of tongues is evidence that one is saved or sanctified. Provide some reasons why speaking in tongues is not an indication of one's salvation or sanctification.

4. Cite some important differences between the modern practice of speaking in tongues and the gift that was exercised in the New Testament.

The Gift of the Holy Spirit in Acts 2:38

"Then Peter said to them, 'Repent, and let every one of you be baptized in the name of Jesus Christ for the remission of sins; and you shall receive the gift of the Holy Spirit. For the promise is to you and to your children, and to all who are afar off, as many as the Lord our God will call'" (Acts 2:38-39).

What is the "gift of the Holy Spirit" in this passage? The answer is important to our understanding of the Holy Spirit and His work in our salvation today. This question is seemingly difficult to answer, but the difficulty is caused by many false ideas and teachings concerning the Holy Spirit. Though somewhat difficult, learning the identity of the gift of the Holy Spirit in Acts 2:38 is not an impossible task.

Among the different answers given to this question are:

> Learning the identity of the gift of the Holy Spirit in Acts 2:38 is not an impossible task.

- A literal indwelling of the Holy Spirit

- A spiritual indwelling of the Holy Spirit through the word of God

- The possession of the miraculous gifts of the Holy Spirit

- The forgiveness of sins and the hope of eternal salvation

One will note that some believe the "gift" is the Holy Spirit Himself, while others believe the "gift" is something given by the Holy Spirit. To make matters more confusing, there is disagreement within these two groups. Those who believe the gift is the Holy Spirit claim Peter is promising a personal indwelling of the Holy Spirit in every Christian. Some claim this happens miraculously, while others claim the Holy Spirit dwells within the Christian through the word of God. Some who claim the gift to be something given by the Holy Spirit believe this promise has reference to the miraculous gifts of the Holy Spirit; the ability to speak in tongues, prophesy, see visions (vv. 4, 17), etc. Others, including myself, believe the gift of the Holy Spirit is "the remission of sins" promised in the same that mentions the gift (Acts 2:38).

All of these answers cannot be correct. However, because this passage is used by some to promote false ideas (a personal, miraculous indwelling of the Holy Spirit, modern day miraculous gifts of the Holy Spirit, etc.), it is important that the Christian study this verse and understand what Peter meant when he promised the "gift of the Holy Spirit" to those who obey the gospel.

The Grammar of the Text

This question is difficult to answer, in part, because the grammar of the text can be understood in different ways.

> "What is the gift of the Holy Spirit in Acts 2:38? Grammatically it may be either the Holy Spirit Himself, or it may be that which the Holy Spirit gives. The grammar does not determine whether the Holy Spirit is the gift or the giver" (Puckett, pp. 12-13).

The grammar does not determine whether the Holy Spirit is the gift or the giver.

Perhaps this difficulty can be better appreciated by looking at some passages in the New Testament that have a similar sentence structure.

> "Jesus answered and said to her, 'If you knew **the gift of God**, and who it is who says to you, "Give Me a drink," you would have asked Him, and He would have given you living water'" (John 4:10; emphasis mine—HR). In this passage, the "gift of God" is that which God gives; the living water.

> "But unto every one of us is given grace according to the measure of **the gift of Christ**" (Eph. 4:7, KJV; emphasis mine—HR). In this passage, the "gift of Christ" is that which Christ gives; the differing gifts possessed by the members of the local church. This meaning is expressed in other translations of the same verse: "Christ's gift" (NKJV, NASB, ESV).

> "And he received **the sign of circumcision**, a seal of the righteousness of the faith which he had while still uncircumcised, that he might be the father of all those who believe, though they are uncircumcised, that righteousness might be imputed to them also" (Rom. 4:11; emphasis mine—HR). This verse has a similar word structure, however, the "sign of circumcision" is not something that circumcision gives; it is actually circumcision.

These examples help us appreciate the fact that the grammar of Acts 2:38 cannot identify the "gift of the Holy

Spirit." To properly identify this gift, we must look at the context of the passage in which the verse is found.

Peter's Sermon in Acts Chapter Two

In Acts chapter two, Jews from different nations had gathered together in the city of Jerusalem to observe the feast of Pentecost. The Holy Spirit fell upon the apostles. The sound of a mighty rushing wind was heard, which drew these Jews together and they heard the apostles speaking in tongues. Some of the Jews understood this to be a sign, and asked what it meant, while others accused the apostles of being drunk (vv. 12-13).

Peter easily answered the accusation of drunkenness and told the Jews they were witnessing the fulfillment of what was promised through the prophet Joel. Acts 2:17-21 is a quotation of Joel 2:28-32. The passage promised the day would come when the Lord would pour forth His Spirit on all flesh, causing sons and daughters to prophesy, see visions, and dream dreams. It also promised the time period would be marked with wonders and signs in heaven and on earth. The climax of the promise is found in the following words—"And it shall come to pass that whoever calls on the name of the Lord shall be saved" (v. 21).

The mention of men being saved led Peter to talk about Jesus. These Jews knew Jesus. His work and teaching had been confirmed by God through the miracles He had performed (v. 22). They delivered Jesus to be crucified, but God raised Him from the dead, as was prophesied in the Old Testament and witnessed by the apostles (vv. 23-32).

Peter then answers their original question asked in verse 12: "Whatever could this mean?" They wanted to know why they were hearing the apostles speak in tongues. Peter said, "Therefore being exalted to the right hand of God, and having received from the Father the promise of the Holy Spirit, He poured out this which you now see and hear" (v. 33). He reminded them that the Christ would be exalted to a position of authority and judgment over His enemies (vv. 34-35), and then concluded by saying, "Therefore let all the house of Israel know assuredly that God has made this Jesus, whom you crucified, both Lord and Christ" (v. 36).

Notice the response on the part of the Jews: "Now when they heard this, they were cut to the heart, and said to

And it shall come to pass in the last days, says God, That I will pour out of My Spirit on all flesh; Your sons and your daughters shall prophesy, Your young men shall see visions, Your old men shall dream dreams. And on My menservants and on My maidservants I will pour out My Spirit in those days; And they shall prophesy.

- Acts 2:17-18

Peter and the rest of the apostles, 'Men and brethren, what shall we do?'" (v. 37). They were cut to the heart because they now realized they had crucified the Son of God and knew they stood condemned before God. When they asked, "What shall we do?" they were not asking how they could receive the Holy Spirit, speak in tongues, and prophesy. Joel had prophesied, "Whoever calls on the name of the Lord shall be saved" (v. 21). They were asking what they had to do to be saved.

Peter answered, "Repent, and let every one of you be baptized in the name of Jesus Christ for the remission of sins; and you shall receive the gift of the Holy Spirit. For the promise is to you and to your children, and to all who are afar off, as many as the Lord our God will call" (vv. 38-39). Peter told them to repent and be baptized for the remission of their sins, and then told them they would receive the gift of the Holy Spirit, which was promised to them, their children, and to all who are afar off. The subject under consideration in the context is salvation. Peter was answering their question about salvation. Why would he add a promise about the indwelling of the Holy Spirit, or the miraculous gifts of the Holy Spirit, in response to a question about salvation?

The context of Acts chapter two argues in favor of the "gift" being something given by the Holy Spirit, not the Holy Spirit Himself. Specifically, it is the gift of the remission of sins—our salvation from sin.

The Promise of the Spirit

The promise in verse 39 is not the miraculous gifts of the Holy Spirit, or the personal indwelling of the Holy Spirit. It is the promise that "whoever calls on the name of the Lord shall be saved" (v. 21).

> Not every Christian in the First Century had the miraculous gifts of the Holy Spirit, yet this promise is made to everyone who repents and is baptized.

This promise was made "to you and to your children, and to all who are afar off, as many as the Lord our God will call" (v. 39). Peter certainly was not speaking of the miraculous gifts of the Holy Spirit in this passage. Not every Christian in the First Century had the miraculous gifts of the Holy Spirit (Rom. 1:11), yet this promise is made to everyone who repents and is baptized. The miraculous gifts were given through the laying on of the hands of an apostle, not at the point of water baptism. Also, the miraculous gifts of the Holy Spirit were only temporary (1 Cor. 13:8-12), while this promise given by Peter is perpetual.

Acts chapter two emphasizes the scope of the promise. Verse 17 says the Spirit would be poured out on "all flesh." Verse 21 says "whoever" calls on the name of the Lord will be saved. Peter concluded that the promise was extended "to all who are afar off, as many as the Lord our God will call" (v. 39). These phrases contain the echo of the promise made to Abraham, Isaac, and Jacob: "In your seed all the nations of the earth shall be blessed" (Gen. 22:18; c.f. 26:4, 28:14).

In Galatians 3:8, Paul quotes Genesis 22:18 and says it was a promise that salvation would be given to all mankind, including the Gentiles—"And the Scripture, foreseeing that God would justify the Gentiles by faith, preached the gospel to Abraham beforehand, saying, 'In you all the nations shall be blessed.'"

Paul goes on to say, "That the blessing of Abraham might come upon the Gentiles in Christ Jesus, that we might receive the promise of the Spirit through faith" (Galatians 3:14). Paul identified something as "the promise of the Spirit." What is this promise? It is not the possession of the miraculous gifts, neither is it the promise of a personal indwelling of the Holy Spirit. It is justification; the forgiveness of sins (vv. 8-14). This is the promise that Abraham and the patriarchs longed for, but did not receive apart from the Gentiles (Heb. 11:13, 17, 39-40). This promise is not received by works of the Law of Moses. It is received by faith; by calling upon the name of the Lord, which Peter defined as repenting and being baptized (Acts 2:38; c.f. Acts 22:16).

Why is the forgiveness of sins called the "gift of the Holy Spirit" and the "promise of the Spirit"? The Holy Spirit played a very important role in securing the forgiveness of our sins and making it available to all mankind. The Holy Spirit inspired the prophets of old who spoke of the coming Messiah. The Holy Spirit worked through the apostles who first preached the gospel, which set forth the terms of salvation. The Holy Spirit inspired the men who wrote the New Testament. To this very day, the forgiveness of sins continues to be a gift that is promised by the Holy Spirit. To receive this gift, we must meet the terms set forth in the gospel.

Conclusion

There are some aspects of the Bible's teaching on the Holy Spirit that are difficult to understand. This is especially true regarding the identity of the gift of the Holy Spirit in Acts

> The forgiveness of sins continues to be a gift that is promised by the Holy Spirit. To receive this gift, we must meet the terms set forth in the gospel.

2:38. As has been shown in our study, it is impossible to answer this question from the grammar of the text. One must look at the context, and consult other passages, and then arrive at a conclusion. The fact that sincere and knowledgeable brethren reach different conclusions regarding this specific question should tell us that it is not easy to understand.

The best understanding of this passage is to identify the gift of the Holy Spirit in Acts 2:38 as the promise of the forgiveness of sins. We have already shown that not all believers in the First Century had the miraculous gifts of the Holy Spirit, so this blessing does not fit the scope of this promise. We have already discussed the indwelling of the Holy Spirit in lesson eight, and have shown that the Holy Spirit does not personally and miraculously dwell in the believer. The gift of the Holy Spirit cannot be the baptismal measure of the Holy Spirit. That was promised to the apostles, not to all mankind (lesson nine). Through the process of elimination, as well as a thorough study of Acts chapter two, we conclude that the gift of the Holy Spirit is the promise of the remission of sins, a promise that continues to be offered every time and everywhere the gospel is preached today.

References

Puckett, Franklin. *The Holy Spirit*. Bowling Green, KY. Guardian of Truth. Print.

Questions

1. Does the grammar of Acts 2:38 determine the meaning of the gift of the Holy Spirit?

    _____

2. What was "the gift of God" in John 4:10? _____

    _____

3. What was "the gift of Christ" in Ephesians 4:7? _____

    _____

4. What prophet did Peter quote in Acts 2:17-21? _____

5. What important promise was given at the conclusion of this prophecy (v. 21)?

    _____

    _____

6. Why were the Jews "cut to the heart" (Acts 2:37)? _____

    _____

    _____

7. What, specifically, were they asking for in verse 37?_____

    _____

8. Discuss some reasons why the gift of the Holy Spirit in Acts 2:38 cannot be the
    miraculous gifts of the Holy Spirit. _____

    _____

    _____

9. What promise was made to Abraham (Gen. 22:18)?_____

    _____

    _____

10. According to Paul, what was "the promise of the Spirit" (Gal. 3:8, 14)?_____

    _____

    _____

11. Why can the forgiveness of sins be called "the gift of the Holy Spirit" or "the promise
    of the Spirit?" _____

    _____

    _____

12. Why do we need to study this matter and understand what is meant by "the gift of
    the Holy Spirit" in Acts 2:38? _____

    _____

    _____

Sins Against the Holy Spirit

In our study we have noted the Holy Spirit is deity. He is an equal member of the Godhead. The Holy Spirit also bears the marks and characteristics of a person. He is not an "it"—a mere force or influence. He is an individual. We have also noted how the Holy Spirit plays an active role in our conversion and our on-going sanctification. He is both interested in and involved in our salvation.

Because of the Holy Spirit's nature and personal involvement in our salvation, it is possible for us to sin against the Holy Spirit. We must take this matter very seriously. Ananias and Sapphira lied to the Holy Spirit and were struck dead (Acts 5:1-5). Let's consider some ways the Bible says we can sin against the Holy Spirit.

The Sin of Resisting the Holy Spirit

Stephen accused the Jews of always resisting the Holy Spirit (Acts 7:51-53). He said their fathers had done this by persecuting the prophets (who were speaking by inspiration of the Spirit) and by not keeping the law (which was delivered by the Spirit). Likewise, these Jews were resisting the Holy Spirit by rejecting the preaching of the apostles and other inspired men and by persecuting the church.

The idea of resisting something means more than simply ignoring it. The word "resist" is translated from a Greek word which means to fall against or upon something. In this sense, to resist is to oppose or strive against something. These Jews were not indifferent about the gospel. They were opposing the gospel with all their might.

The same Holy Spirit who inspired the prophets of old also inspired the apostles who wrote the New Testament. Today, one resists the Holy Spirit when he rejects and opposes the message of the New Testament.

The Sin of Quenching the Holy Spirit

"Do not quench the Spirit. Do not despise prophecies" (1 Thess. 5:19-20).

> You stiff-necked and uncircumcised in heart and ears! You always resist the Holy Spirit; as your fathers did, so do you.
>
> - Acts 7:51

The Greek word rendered "quench" in this passage means "to extinguish." Every time this word is used in the New Testament it refers to the act of quenching a fire or things on fire (literally or metaphorically). As used in this verse, the word means to quench, suppress, or stifle a divine influence.

The Thessalonians were not to despise the prophecies made by those who had this gift (v. 20). To ignore these prophecies would be to extinguish the work the Holy Spirit was doing among them.

Timothy had a miraculous gift of the Holy Spirit. Likening this gift to a fire, Paul issued two warnings to Timothy concerning this gift. Instead of neglecting the gift (like letting a fire die out—1 Tim. 4:14), and he was to stir it up (like stoking a fire—2 Tim. 1:6; see the verse in the English Standard Version). Otherwise, Timothy would have been quenching the Holy Spirit with regard to the gift he had been given.

The Holy Spirit works through His word, pricking men's hearts (Acts 2:37) and causing them to burn (Luke 24:32). Whenever the impact of the word of God is ignored, the Holy Spirit has been quenched. When we stop reading the word and praying for God's help, we have quenched the Holy Spirit's intended influence upon our lives.

> And they said to one another, "Did not our heart burn within us while He talked with us on the road, and while He opened the Scriptures to us?"
>
> - Luke 24:32

The Sin of Grieving the Holy Spirit

"And do not grieve the Holy Spirit of God, by whom you were sealed for the day of redemption" (Eph. 4:30).

These Christians were told not to grieve the Holy Spirit. To "grieve" means to make one sorrowful, to cause someone to suffer with grief or sadness. How is it possible for a Christian to bring sorrow to the Holy Spirit? This warning is given in the context of Christians being told to put off the corrupt conduct of their former lives and to put on the new man who has been created in righteousness and holiness (vv. 22-24). Paul goes on to specifically address their speech, anger, work habits, generosity, as well as various attitudes (vv. 25-32).

When we fail to live the way God has told us to live, we have rejected God's authority for our lives. Such rebellion causes the Holy Spirit to experience deep sorrow, much like the parents of a wayward and foolish child (Prov. 10:1, 17:25). Any time we disobey God and violate the commands given by the Holy Spirit, we grieve the Holy Spirit.

The Sin of Insulting the Holy Spirit

In Hebrews 10:26-29, the writer speaks of those who sin willfully, understanding what they are doing, without showing any desire to repent. Such persons are said to have "insulted" the Spirit of grace, or to have "done despite unto the Spirit of grace" (KJV).

The word "insulted" is translated from a Greek word which means to insult, but it also carries with it the idea of acting with contempt. It describes one who is haughty and thus acts against the authority of another, the result of which is a scornful insult to the one in the position of authority. This attitude is exactly what is described in the above passage.

When a Christian sins willfully, he has taken the Son of God, whom God has exalted highly (Phil. 2:9), and has brought Him down to the level of dirt to be walked upon and has regarded His blood to be a common thing. For a man, who is the object of God's grace, who has been cleansed in the blood that made this grace possible, and has received this grace through the working of the Holy Spirit, to treat Christ in this way is the worst insult that can be given to the Holy Spirit.

We insult the Holy Spirit when we sin willfully, rejecting God's efforts to save our soul, without showing any desire to repent. Such a person can expect a certain and fearful judgment. One cannot disregard the blood of Christ and insult the Spirit of grace without falling into the hands of the living God (Heb. 10:31).

The Sin of Blasphemy Against the Holy Spirit

"Therefore I say to you, every sin and blasphemy will be forgiven men, but the blasphemy against the Spirit will not be forgiven men. Anyone who speaks a word against the Son of Man, it will be forgiven him; but whoever speaks against the Holy Spirit, it will not be forgiven him, either in this age or in the age to come" (Matt. 12:31-32).

Many people have troubled themselves over the possibility of committing the unpardonable sin of blaspheming the Holy Spirit. The word "blaspheme" is translated from a Greek word which means to speak against someone in an effort to harm or injure their name. To understand the meaning of what Jesus called "the blasphemy against the Holy Spirit" one must look at the context in which this warning was given.

Instructions regarding the blasphemy of the Holy Spirit are found in three passages in the New Testament: Matthew 12:31-32; Mark 3:28-30; Luke 12:10.

- vv. 22-24—Jesus healed a demon-possessed man. His enemies could not deny a miracle had taken place, but instead credited the miracle to the working of Satan.

- vv. 25-27—Jesus showed their charge was absurd. No man can work against himself and hope for his effort to stand. Also, their own people cast out demons, and they could testify that demons are not cast out by the power of Satan.

- vv. 28-29—Jesus indicated His ability to cast out these demons was evidence the kingdom of God had come upon them and His kingdom was more powerful than the kingdom of Satan.

- vv. 31-32—The warning against blaspheming the Holy Spirit was given in the context of men rejecting the power of the Lord and the claims that were backed up by this exercise of power.

These Jews were blaspheming "the Son of Man" in that they were dismissing His claims by crediting His works to the power of Satan. Jesus said they could reject Him and still receive the forgiveness of their sins. This was because one more opportunity to hear and repent was coming through the work of the Holy Spirit (who was poured forth on Pentecost—Acts 2), but if they rejected the Holy Spirit, there would not be another opportunity for them to receive the forgiveness of their sins.

This is illustrated in Acts chapter two. When Peter was preaching the first gospel sermon, he told the Jews they had rejected and killed the Son of God (vs. 23, 36), yet they received forgiveness when they obeyed the gospel that was given through the inspiration of the Holy Spirit (v. 33, 38, 41). They did not blaspheme the Holy Spirit (reject the gospel given through the Spirit) but believed, obeyed, and were forgiven.

The sin of blasphemy against the Holy Spirit is not confined to a word that is spoken against the Holy Spirit. It is not a specific sin such as murder or adultery. It is the action of rejecting God's final means of offering salvation to the world—the Gospel of Jesus Christ, inspired by Holy Spirit.

Those who have become so bold as to reject the evidence for God's existence, the reality of their sin, the appeal made through the gospel, and any concern for their

> The sin of blasphemy against the Holy Spirit is the action of rejecting God's final means of offering salvation to the world—the Gospel of Jesus Christ, inspired by Holy Spirit.

soul's salvation, and thus persist in sin, are blaspheming the Holy Spirit. There is no forgiveness for such a person because they reject God's offer of forgiveness.

Some people are concerned about having committed the "unforgivable sin." There is no "unforgivable sin" in the sense that God refuses to forgive a particular sin. The Bible says if we repent and confess our sin, God is faithful and just to forgive us of our sins and to cleanse us of all unrighteousness (1 John 1:9). A sin becomes "unforgivable" when we refuse to accept the truth of the gospel and meet the conditions of forgiveness set forth in the word of God.

Conclusion

Apostasy does not happen overnight. It is a process. It begins when we decide to resist the Holy Spirit (stop reading the Bible and praying). This leads to our quenching the Spirit. A neglect of God's word will result in sins which grieve the Spirit. Soon we become hardened and sin willfully, which insults the Spirit. If repentance is not forthcoming, our heart will be completely hardened, and we will find ourselves blaspheming the Spirit and rejecting everything connected with God. The way we prevent such apostasy in our life is to make sure we are not guilty of sinning against the Holy Spirit, but continue to allow the Spirit to work in our life through His word.

Questions

1. How were the Jews resisting the Holy Spirit (Acts 7:51-53)? _____

    _____

    _____

2. How does one resist the Holy Spirit today? _____

    _____

    _____

3. What warnings did Paul give Timothy regarding his spiritual gift (1 Tim. 4:14; 2 Tim. 1:6)? _____

    _____

4. How does one quench the Holy Spirit today? _____

    _____

    _____

5. What does it mean to grieve a person? _____

    _____

6. How does one grieve the Holy Spirit today? _____

_____

_____

7. How does one insult or do despite to the Holy Spirit today?_____

_____

_____

8. Why is the Holy Spirit insulted when we sin willfully?_____

_____

_____

9. What happens to the person who disregards the blood of Christ and insults the Spirit of grace (Heb. 10:29-31)? _____

_____

_____

10. What does the word "blaspheme" mean?_____

_____

_____

11. How were the scribes and Pharisees blaspheming Jesus Christ (Matt. 12:24; Mark 3:22, 30)?_____

_____

12. How does one blaspheme the Holy Spirit today?_____

_____

_____